moving
through
grief

moving
through
grief

Proven Techniques for Finding Your Way After Any Loss

Gretchen Kubacky, PsyD

ROCKRIDGE PRESS

Interior and Cover Designer: Jami Spittler
Art Producer: Hillary Frileck
Editor: Nora Spiegel
Production Manager: Martin Worthington
Production Editor: Melissa Edeburn
Author photo courtesy of © Cathryn Farnsworth

ISBN: Print 978-1-64152-503-9 | Ebook 978-1-64152-504-6

R0

For everyone who struggles with grief and loss
and who wants to find peace and joy again

Contents

A Roadmap Through Grief

We all experience loss at some point. This book lights a path through the pain. In this book, you'll learn effective ways of coping—ways that can help you move through grief. You'll learn how to stay present in the moment, how to show up in relationships, and how to move toward making your dreams come true.

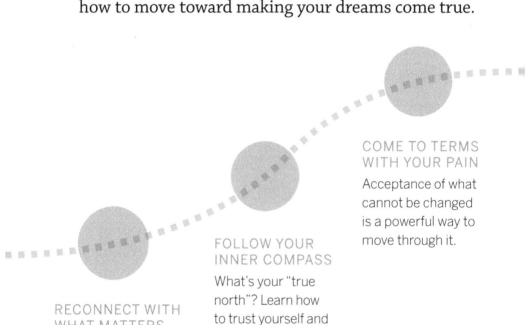

COME TO TERMS WITH YOUR PAIN
Acceptance of what cannot be changed is a powerful way to move through it.

FOLLOW YOUR INNER COMPASS
What's your "true north"? Learn how to trust yourself and let go of thoughts that aren't serving you.

RECONNECT WITH WHAT MATTERS
What matters to you? Home? Family? Money? Health? Create a personalized plan.

LIVE A RICH, FULFILLING LIFE

The net result is not only finding relief from grief but also gaining tools that will serve you well for the rest of your life.

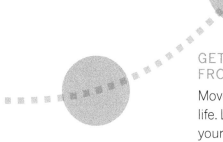

GET UNSTUCK FROM PAIN

Move freely through life. Live according to your values and goals.

SHOW UP FOR YOUR LIFE

When you know what you want, you can set goals for the future you desire.

The Loss That Changed My Life

When I was 13, my father died unexpectedly. My family didn't "do emotions," so we pushed our grief away and quickly got on with our lives. My mom got a job and a boyfriend, I went back to school, and we cried in private. In public, it looked like nothing was wrong, even though everything had changed. None of my friends had lost a parent, and I had no role models for how to grieve. I thought I was doing all right. In retrospect, I was in deep psychological pain and had very few coping skills.

When I went off to college, I began to feel depressed and anxious. I had a hard time being present in relationships. I was fearful that anyone I liked or loved would die, too, so I didn't get close to anyone. I saw a therapist at the college counseling center and talked about my father's passing. She helped me work through the old feelings, and I joined a grief and loss support group. Thankfully, I was able to develop better skills for coping with the grief that life inevitably holds.

Although your loss is your own, your experience of grief may be like the experience of others. Everything you're feeling—an overwhelming sense of anger, despair, hopelessness, or even near paralysis—is normal. You are not going crazy.

Personally, I had a lot of fear, shame, and anxiety at first. But I found supportive people—people who understood grief—and I learned tools for moving through my loss. I developed a strong belief in my capacity not only to cope, but also to grow through grieving. Eventually, this belief led to my career as a psychologist and certified bereavement facilitator.

Today, I want to share my tools and strategies with you, so that your life can be better and less painful. You don't have to let go of who or what you loved and miss, but you do have a choice now—a choice to become more resilient, happier, and healthier.

How to Use This Book

The most helpful way to approach this book is to work through it from beginning to end. Each chapter builds on the one before, allowing you to learn new coping skills quickly and easily. Have a notebook or journal handy for writing reflections and doing other exercises.

Reading about new skills is one thing, but there's nothing more powerful than jumping in and trying them for yourself. Throughout this book, you'll find practical activities everywhere you see the phrase "Try This." These skill builders will help you understand and assimilate new concepts as they are explained. For example, you'll explore and write about what you value most, and you will develop a step-by-step plan to put your ideas into practice.

Feeling overwhelmed and unmotivated is common for people struggling with grief. Promise yourself that you will get through the book at least once. Of course, the pacing is entirely up to you. Be gentle with yourself. Pause when you need to. But know this: Steady work leads to steady progress. The more you embrace the concepts and practice them using the tools in this book, the more you will improve. As your successes become more frequent, you'll find yourself living a happier, fuller, and richer life in which anything is possible—even joy.

CHAPTER 1

Living with Loss

When most people think of grief, they think of deep sorrow over the death of a loved one, but grief takes many forms. You might experience grief from the loss of a job or a home, or from cumulative losses like the loss of health through chronic illness or the loss of your time and youth. Relationships and life changes have different meaning for different people. You might think you're a capable driver and find yourself questioning that after you cause a car crash. Or someone might break up with you and, even if you were thinking about breaking up with them anyway, it still feels surprisingly sad. Sometimes, we grieve our hopes or fantasies—a friendship that never developed, a romance that never went past the third date, or a project that never came to fruition.

Loss of an Important Relationship

The death of (or estrangement from) your spouse or partner, a family member, or a dear friend or colleague is probably one of the hardest types of loss to deal with because our relationships define our lives. Adult children who have lost both parents often say they feel like orphans. Loss of a close friend can feel just as painful as the loss of a family member. Loss of a colleague who was a mentor can leave us feeling rudderless.

For many, the death of a beloved pet is even more profound than the loss of a human companion. Our animal friends transcend loneliness, bad moods, and discomfort. The loss of their unconditional love and affection often leaves us feeling deeply bereft.

Illness

Whether acute or prolonged, both chronic and terminal illnesses can result in innumerable losses. You lose not only your health, but also your sense of safety, peace, and happiness. In a way, you lose the ability to relax—to not think about your body. You may lose friends who can't handle your illness or face your death. You may lose your financial security or your ability to live independently. You may even lose parts of your body to chemotherapy or surgery.

A serious mental health diagnosis may leave you feeling like you've "lost your mind." If you have brain fog, fatigue, mental confusion, or a more serious diagnosis, you may feel that you have lost the respect of others as well as hope for yourself.

Disability or Loss of Ability

Disability or loss of ability can be visible or invisible, physical or psychological. Chronic illness can be depleting, leaving you with little energy or interest to engage with friends. Anxiety may make you scared to leave the house, particularly if you have balance and stability problems or need to take medication before you eat. Although some people don't want to deal with the kinds of accommodations you need to be fully part of life, more people are kind, generous, and understanding.

Change in Employment Status

The loss of a career is stressful, whether because of a layoff, a forced retirement, failure to get a promotion or to gain admission to a requisite program of study, or an undesirable job or location transfer. Having to shut down a business you founded can be a crushing blow. Loss of economic security can also cause grief.

Other Causes of Grief

Many other forms of loss may seem less significant, but if experienced in a short time frame, they can add up to a significant experience of grief. You may be coping—and then, suddenly, you're not. Here are a few more losses that can lead to grief:

+ Loss of a loved one to alcohol or drug use, incarceration, military deployment, serious illness, or dementia

+ Loss of a home to a disaster or financial troubles and loss of security through a home invasion

+ Loss of the familiar world after graduating college, receiving a promotion, moving homes, or becoming a parent

+ Miscarriage, premature infant death, and infertility

+ Loss of control or sense of safety due to political unrest, climate change, economic upheaval, and terrorism

+ Loss of identity or a sense of belonging through divorce or when children grow up and leave the home

TRY THIS: Describe What You Have Lost

It's time to begin your first reflective writing exercise, which will explore your own experience of loss. Or, as I often say, it's time to "cozy up" to your grief.

Find a comfortable, private space and block out some quiet time. Get out your notebook or laptop. A box of tissues might be helpful, too. Skip the glass of wine—it might sound soothing, but drinking alcohol is counterproductive to letting your real thoughts and feelings flow.

Take a few minutes to reflect on your primary loss—the one that brought you to this book. If it helps, use the following questions as jumping-off points. Don't worry about neatness, grammar, spelling, or whether what you're writing makes sense. Give yourself permission to say whatever you need to say, unedited. This journal is for your eyes only.

- As a result of your primary loss, what else did you lose? Other people? Future experiences or activities? Your sense of safety or belonging?

- What emotional experiences have you lost? Joy? Love? Satisfaction?

- How would getting any of these things back feel?

Finish by thanking yourself for taking the first steps toward moving through your grief.

What This Book Will Do for You

Thinking about the many ways that loss can affect you can be overwhelming. Grief can be crushing, like a heavily weighted blanket holding you down. You may feel like you can't move, and dark thoughts can follow quickly. It's hard to know where to begin, and just thinking about ending this constant sadness doesn't cut it. You know you've got to take action—but what action?

What if I told you that grief didn't have to be so awfully heavy and prolonged? What if grief could even become a gift? If you're intrigued by the idea that loss can be transformed into joy—that grief can make you healthier, stronger, and happier—read on. I've got an entirely different approach to moving through grief that is based on decades of ideas proven to be effective and that is rooted in psychological research on grief and suffering. This approach will take some effort, and a little patience, but it works.

This book will show you how to get back to living the full, rich life that you deserve. You'll learn to develop psychological flexibility—a different way of thinking about who or what you've lost and about what is possible in the future. Once you learn this approach, you will become better able to adapt to difficult and painful situations. There's an old saying that "Pain is inevitable; suffering is optional." It's true: You can't erase pain, but you can change how you relate to it.

We're going to start by reconnecting you with your personal goals and values—the things that you were committed to before your loss.

Once you have an idea of what you want, you can begin focusing on the people and activities that bring you happiness. Eventually, these "joy points" diminish the pain. Consistently nurturing your joy points will change the wiring in your brain, increasing your motivation. You will start showing up to your life again.

Anytime you feel numb with grief, pick up this book. You won't be retreating into the background and waiting for things to get better, easier, or less sad—you'll be doing something to get yourself unstuck. Everything in this book is designed with one goal: connecting you with the life you want. You'll know that you can manage grief, rather than letting grief weigh you down, and that is a powerful feeling.

This book is not a miracle cure for grief; nothing is. Rather, it provides an actionable and effective step-by-step plan for relieving grief and sadness, regardless of the cause. This plan is based on acceptance and commitment therapy (ACT), and it will help you both accept the reality of post–loss life and develop a healthier context for this reality. Your loss will become a part of your life, not something that takes all of your energy. You won't waste time trying to suppress your grief. You will transform your relationship with it.

Are you ready?

What Is ACT?

Created by psychologist Dr. Steven C. Hayes in 1982, ACT is a practical set of techniques for developing psychological flexibility. Widely used and evidence based, with hundreds of studies documenting its effectiveness according to the Association for Contextual Behavioral Science, ACT is an approach that encourages us to mindfully embrace the things that trouble us. Such acceptance means becoming the observer of your own thoughts, allowing them to come and go without judgment. There are no true or false thoughts, merely thoughts that are helpful and thoughts that are not. ACT facilitates the development of skills and capacities that can help you thrive. By ceasing to fight grief and by making a commitment to behavioral changes, you increase your resilience and your grief naturally recedes.

ACT is uniquely suited to the grieving process because it helps you learn to live in spite of, or alongside, grief.

HOW ACT IS USED IN THIS PROGRAM

ACT uses six tools: values, committed action, acceptance, being present, cognitive defusion, and self-as-context. Think of them as the tools in your toolbox. Each is indispensable, and doesn't work very well if it's not used properly. Say you want to frame and hang a picture. If you try to "saw" wood for a frame with pliers, you'll end up with jagged, imprecise edges. And if you use those same pliers to pound a nail into the wall, you're probably going to hurt your hand and mess up your wall in the process. If you choose the proper tools upfront—a saw for sawing, and a hammer for nailing—then your job will be quick and easy. With framing pictures as with ACT, there are lots of tools, and you need to know the specific purpose of each to use them effectively. For now, here's a brief summary of how the ACT tools will be covered in the chapters to come.

Values

Your values are what matter to you—what you choose to prioritize as meaningful. Grieving may bring up memories of ignoring or acting contrary to your values, resulting in feelings of unhappiness or unful-fillment. Without the cornerstone of your values, you will drift into dissatisfaction and frustration.

When you know your values, you can make the best choices for yourself. In moments of uncertainty, you can use your values as your personal compass. As you begin to focus on values-guided living, you may identify many desired changes you'd like to make in your life.

In chapter 2, "Reconnecting with What Matters," you will explore and clarify your values, which you will use as the basis for working through future chapters and challenges.

Committed Action

You can bring your values into your day-to-day life by committing to goals and actions—to "living your values" in the wake of loss. Committed action is the process of moving toward change by defining what you want most, figuring out the necessary steps to get there, and honoring your intentions by executing the plan. For example, if you value family time, you might commit to spending quality time with your baby sister. Prioritizing your values and setting values-based goals leads to an immediate reduction in anxiety. It strips away mental chatter—all those thoughts and beliefs that run on an endless loop in your brain—allowing you to direct your energies toward the things that matter.

Chapter 3, "Following Your Inner Compass," will show you how to translate your values into readily achievable short-term goals, immediately starting you off on a path to living a life aligned with your values.

Acceptance

If your grief brings up dark and intense emotions, you might struggle to put one foot in front of the other, let alone follow through on long-term goals.

Acceptance is a powerful antidote to avoidance. It requires acknowledging troubling emotions, without judging or taking action to counteract them. Feelings are not facts; they are just information. When you allow yourself to stop judging your grief, you may realize that you're not actually feeling what you thought you were feeling, but rather what you thought you were *supposed* to be feeling. For example, if you believe outward suffering is necessary to prove that you love someone who died, you will act quite differently than someone who holds another set of beliefs. And if you're not having the experience your mind tells you that you should be having—if you think you're grieving "incorrectly"—you may feel confused, guilty, or ashamed.

You may not be that sad when you lose a job you secretly hated but believed that you should be grateful for and committed to. Similarly, you may be fine with the end to a relationship that wasn't working. Other people's ideas don't matter here—only the ideas you have, as they relate to your chosen values. We can make choices that help us live more fully and authentically by treating our thoughts and beliefs as information rather than fact.

In chapter 4, "Coming to Terms with Pain," you will explore ways to meet your grief with true acceptance—not by surrendering or giving in, but by actively choosing to accept both ups and downs—and, consequently, to continue taking committed action.

Being Present

In our high-pitched, distraction-filled culture, simply being present is becoming increasingly difficult. Demands on our attention lead to increased anxiety, fear, and distress. You can counteract these forces by slowing down and bringing awareness to everyday activities, such as walking the dog, washing the dishes, or folding clothes. By choosing to focus your thoughts on the present moment, you will activate the parasympathetic nervous system—the body's built-in leveling device. Mindful movement and meditation exercises are also part of bringing your mind and body into alignment with the present moment.

In chapter 5, "Showing Up for Your Life," you'll focus on how to be present even when you want to retreat into the past or adopt behaviors that compromise your mental health and psychological functioning.

Our mindful, observing selves can discern which thoughts serve our well-being and deserve attention. Imagine your mind is a bus. You're the driver, and all of your thoughts are passengers. Each passenger competes for your attention, and yet, as the driver, you're in charge. You can keep moving forward while choosing which of the passengers will receive your attention. That's cognitive defusion.

Self-as-context means viewing yourself as the central character in a story, for example, "Hopeless Joe" or "Worthless Annie." By creating a new personal label, you can become an independent observer of the story.

In chapter 6, "You Are Bigger Than Your Sadness," you'll learn several ways to practice becoming the observer.

Remember that "feeling better" is not the goal of ACT. You don't need to wait until you feel less sad, angry, or frightened to start making real progress in your life.

IF YOU NEED MORE SUPPORT

This book is no substitute for professional mental health assessment or treatment. If you feel overwhelmed or suicidal, seek professional help. Here are some warning signs that you need professional help immediately:

- Thinking about dying or looking for a way to end your own life

- Feeling trapped and hopeless, like you have no purpose in life

- Fantasizing about joining the person you lost in the afterlife

- Believing that people would be better off without you

- Experiencing unbearable pain

- Thinking you are a burden to others

- Sleeping too much or too little

- Eating too much or not enough

- Using drugs and alcohol to numb the pain

- Withdrawing or feeling isolated

- Experiencing extreme mood swings

- Having a hard time thinking clearly

Continued

If you are feeling suicidal right now, or if suicide sometimes seems like a reasonable choice, call the National Suicide Prevention Hotline at (800) 273-8255 or text TALK to 741-741. Compassionate and well-trained people staff the hotline 24 hours a day, seven days a week, 365 days a year. You can also call 9-1-1 or head to your nearest emergency room. Don't waste time posting a message on social media, hoping someone will notice. Feeling suicidal is always an emergency, and you are worth saving.

If you're not feeling suicidal right now, but still need additional support, you can find a skilled grief therapist by searching for referrals at https://www.psychologytoday.com/us/therapists.

TAKEAWAYS

+ Grief can be caused by death or many other types of loss.

+ *Moving Through Grief* offers scientifically proven ACT skills to help change how you experience grief and increase psychological flexibility and resilience.

+ Writing in a journal can help you think through your feelings about loss.

+ Changing your relationship with grief and loss will improve your quality of life.

+ You can have a rich and fulfilling life after loss.

+ You don't have to "get over it" to have a better life.

CHAPTER 2

Reconnecting with What Matters

The Big Idea: Your Values

Values are your personal ideals. Only you define your values—you create them for yourself and they are uniquely yours. They are not goals that you eventually accomplish; rather, they are guideposts for your life. Whereas goals can be listed and achieved (marriage, for example), values are ideals toward which you're always moving (a loving relationship, for example). Values help you act with intention and a clear sense of purpose.

Values can guide your interactions with the world and other people, the way you choose to spend your time, and the way you treat yourself. By simplifying life, on your own terms, you have a much greater chance of taking the meaningful actions that you need to live your best life, and you will naturally feel happier, more productive, and more satisfied.

Your values provide inspiration, motivation, and direction, and they increase commitment. They may also be aspirational—assertiveness, authenticity, courageousness, flexibility, gratitude, honesty, and trustworthiness, for example. They underlie every choice and every action. Adhering to your values can guide you toward a life that is rich with purpose, meaning, and satisfaction.

As you start to think about your values, ask yourself how your life could improve. Consider what you will show the world by living according to your values. Think about what it will feel like to set and accomplish goals inspired by your values.

Clarifying your values allows you to be clearer in your communication with others. You will spend less time doing things that make other people happy and more time doing things that bring you closer to your goals. Instead of living behind a mask or by someone else's rules, you will live authentically.

Values are like a compass pointing you to true north when you are struggling with grief from loss.

TRY THIS: Clarify Your Values

This exercise will help you clarify your values in relation to multiple aspects of your life, such as family, romantic relationships, friends, work, spirituality, health, education, recreation, sexuality, community, environment, parenting, and citizenship.

You will need your journal or laptop. Answer the following questions in as much detail as you can. Let your writing flow in a stream of consciousness, without editing (there will be time for that later) and without judgment.

+ What were the most important things in your life before your loss?

+ Who were the most important people in your life?

+ What is one big thing you want to accomplish in your life?

+ What do you imagine your life looking like in the future?

+ At your funeral, what would you want to be remembered for?

+ What life experiences have left you feeling the happiest?

+ What sort of relationships would you like to build with family and friends?

+ How do you want other people to see and experience you?

+ What kind of life would you create if you could live the life you wanted?

+ What kind of work would feel meaningful to you?

+ How would you like to contribute to the world?

If you want to explore further, answer these questions:

+ Is some form of spirituality important to you?

+ What kind of person would you need to be to create meaningful change in the world?

+ How do you want to look after your health?

Read what you wrote and highlight key words, those that occur several times and those that describe personal characteristics. These words will help you clarify your values.

How Your Values Will Help

Values-guided action is the core of ACT. Values are used to help you stay in touch with the reason you are making change. Without meaning and purpose, action is aimless. And although action without focus will certainly keep you busy, it won't get you what you want. It may even leave you feeling adrift in a sea of choices. After a loss, it's tempting to act as quickly as possible. We want to fix things. We want to get out of our pain as quickly as possible. After a job loss, we immediately apply for every job that we minimally qualify for. After we get dumped, we may immediately start dating again, without taking time to analyze what went wrong in the relationship or whether it was even aligned with our key values.

Values are also freely chosen. Trying to orient your life around someone else's values doesn't work—maybe you've already tried this and know from experience. Your parents, your spouse, or your boss should not be driving your personal values. As you look at your list of values, remember that only those that resonate will stick.

As important as values may be, they produce change only when coupled with mindful and ongoing action. Values remind you of your purpose. They serve as an anchor, keeping you from going adrift as you embrace the work of moving through grief.

For people who are dealing with a major loss, values serve as a compass, pointing you to your chosen direction and helping you determine what changes to make. If you doubt a particular action, ask yourself: "Is this action aligned with my values?" If you determine that the action is not aligned with your values, don't take it. If the action does seem to be aligned with your values, you can move forward with clarity and confidence.

The constancy of your values (unlike the future orientation of goals) allows you to stay in the present moment and to make decisions that will ultimately lead to a happier future. If you're afraid that you can't make good decisions because of your grief, remember your values. Your activities and behaviors might change, but your core values won't.

Values are inherently relationship based because they affect the people in our lives or the world in general. By consistently adhering to your values, you build and reinforce your relationships. No one can ever replace a lost loved one. But ACT can help you embrace the impermanence of life.

Through nurturing, other relationships can become the glue that fills the cracks, holding the broken pieces of your life together. These relationships can ease damage, loss, and transition by bringing joy.

TRY THIS: Get Closer to What Matters

You have already defined some of your values; now, create a vision of those values in action. Start by writing the words you highlighted in the previous journaling exercise. Refer to them as you answer these questions:

+ Personal Growth: What are your strengths? What would you like to have more of?

+ Health: What are the main characteristics of a healthy body and mind?

+ Leisure: Do you like being creative? Productive? What brings you joy and pleasure?

+ Work: What were you taught about work, and what do you believe now? Do you have work-life balance?

+ Wealth: If you were gifted one million dollars today, what would you do with it? Spend it on fun? Pay off debt? Help others? How does your choice reflect on you?

+ Family: What were your proclaimed versus unspoken family values? How can you build on those values?

+ Social: What kind of friend do you want to be? What kind of friends do you attract?

+ Community: What do you stand for? If you were running for political office, how would others characterize you?

+ Environment: What is your commitment to the planet and other people?

Answer the following questions if they apply to you:

+ Parenting: What values, dreams, and achievements do you want to transfer to your children? How do you want them to remember you?

+ Intimacy: What do you value about your relationship? How do you and your partner treat each other?

+ Spirituality: How do your spiritual beliefs inspire you? What are you rejecting or embracing?

Meeting Your Grief with Values

Grief is one of the biggest life disruptors imaginable. It tends to leave you feeling paralyzed, confused, and irritable. Nothing seems to work quite right anymore, and you don't know what is most important. How can you make good decisions when you are overwhelmed by loss?

Rather than withdrawing, losing motivation, and avoiding important activities, focus on values that will guide you toward choices that get you engaged in life, connected with people, and away from things that worsen your hurt. Transform the "yes but" approach to the "yes and" approach.

"Yes but" feels like an attack:

+ "I like your dress, but that purse . . ."

+ "You did a great job on the first part of the report, but . . ."

+ "I think you're a really great guy, but . . ."

"Yes and" instills confidence and communicates engagement:

+ "I like your dress, and that purse is a really creative choice."

+ "You did a great job on the first part of the report, and I'm looking forward to seeing your next stab at the second part."

+ "I think you're a really great guy, and it's the wrong time for me to be getting into a relationship."

ACT is a "yes and" approach. It acknowledges pain and the benefit of engagement with life. It's not judgmental. It doesn't require you to give up anything else. It asks you to continually evaluate your options in light of your values and to commit to action aligned with those values.

It might be hard to believe that something as simple as choosing your values will result in positive changes--especially if you feel overwhelmed, hopeless, and skeptical of anything that promises to relieve your suffering. This is where ACT is so powerful for grievers: It's not about doing something so you will feel better. You can have all the space and time you need to feel your feelings. No one is going to attack your grief or try to take it away from you.

This process is powerful because it interrupts the well-practiced cycle of your thoughts. Having the same thoughts over and over again won't change your grief—this cycle probably just makes you feel worse. After my father's death, I repeatedly questioned myself: "Why didn't I notice the signs? Why wasn't I with him that night? How could this happen?" I was caught in an obsessive spin cycle of self-doubt and suffering that I could not think myself out of.

The more we lean on our values, the more they become our focus, even when old automatic thoughts—the kind that only serve to trap you in your misery—crop up. Think of ACT as a friend walking beside you, gently pressing you on the elbow to steer you in the right direction if you start to veer off course. If you trust your friend, and believe that your values are sound, you will experience a sense of safety and relief as you move forward.

YOU DON'T NEED TO "GET OVER IT"

"She's in a better place now." "It was God's will." "You guys weren't even married." "A miscarriage isn't like you lost a real baby." "At least he had a long life." "There's a reason for everything." "You'll get over it." "There's something better waiting for you."

How many such comments have you heard from some well-meaning person? Sure, they try, but their comments are invalidating and hurtful. They can cause you to stop sharing. Worse yet, they can reinforce problematic thoughts—that your grieving should be over, you should get over it, you did something wrong.

Give yourself permission to stop trying to get over it. You don't have to get over it, now or ever. You can't will yourself to get over it anyway. Take as long as you need. Just keeping moving forward with your values as a guide. Allow yourself to be less than perfect, because truly, there is no such thing as a perfect grieving process. Grief is messy. Do the best you can. That is all that is required.

TRY THIS: Flip the Script on Your Inner Meanie

Your words are powerful co-creators of your thoughts. Just as you can use them to make yourself feel bad, you can also use them to make yourself feel good. Pull out your journal, and rewrite some scripts.

We've all got an inner meanie who says terrible things to us. Channel that meanie—use all the bad words and negative ideas—and get playful. Start by writing down at least six statements that you think are true about grief. Then write down at least six more that are unique to your particular loss.

Now take those statements and flip the script. When you change the words—and your perspective—you change what's "true." Here are a few examples:

> **Meanie:** You need to put this behind you as quickly as possible.
>
> **Flip it:** I know it's okay for me to take as much time as I need. There's no time limit on grief.
>
> **Meanie:** You're weak.
>
> **Flip it:** I'm sad, and it's okay to feel this way. Feeling my feelings is actually a strength.
>
> **Meanie:** You should be grateful she didn't suffer longer.
>
> **Flip it:** I didn't want her to suffer, and I'm grateful she is at peace. I have every right to be sad about her being gone.

Now read all of the "flip it" statements out loud. Feel their power.

If you're comfortable, type or record all of your flipped statements on your phone. Listen to or read these statements several times a day.

Moving Forward with Values

This program may not immediately lead to less sadness or anxiety, but over time and with consistent action, it will move you toward the kind of life you want to be living. This program will get you unstuck from the grief that's been holding you back. I'm asking you to have a little faith in your own capacity for healing. We all have this capacity. In the moments when you are grieving hard, try to focus on hope—even just the tiniest bit of hope—so that you can keep going.

I sometimes ask: "Can you find just 1 percent of hope?" For now, 1 percent will do. The act of moving forward while having a little hope is valuable. People who keep trying often have sudden leaps and bounds of growth. They wake up one day and realize that things are a lot better, which generates a sense of accomplishment that fuels their desire to keep going.

As hope grows, you may find that the priority of your individual values shifts. If you're grieving the death of a family member, family might initially be your highest-priority value. But when you're feeling better, you might shift your attention to other values. Similarly, if you're dealing with the grief of a serious new medical diagnosis, health may be your highest-priority value. When you've gotten through the initial shock of the diagnosis and aren't desperately trying to learn a new self-care routine, you might refocus on leisure, family, or work.

Some values may never move to the top of your priority list yet will remain a consistently positive force in your life. A relationship that you invest in regularly with quality time and attention can be that force. So, too, can other values, such as daily exercise and meditation—routines that can support you as you devote more attention to other aspects of your life.

I recommend choosing no more than three values to focus on at any given time, so that you can give them the kind of attention that will really move you forward. This next journaling exercise will help you prioritize your values.

You will need your journal for this exercise and the list of values you created earlier. Write down your list of values. If you have more than 10 values, combine some related values into one value. Don't take too much time with this part; rely on your intuition.

Now, take a few minutes to consider how you want to live your life, the things you want to spend your time on, how you want to feel, the people you want to be around, and the activities that bring you joy or satisfaction. Imagine that nothing stands in your way, and don't worry about how you will get there.

Using a scale from 0 (not important) to 10 (highest priority), rate each value. It's okay to have several items with the same score.

Now rewrite your list, putting the highest-priority items at the top. The top three are what we'll focus on first. If you have more than three with the same score, choose the ones you wrote down first.

If you're feeling inspired, write a paragraph or two about your top three values.

Allowing Your Change to Happen

People who are experiencing grief often have many of the same symptoms as people with depression, and can engage in behaviors that make things worse, for example, eating, drinking, or sleeping too much and isolating themselves from friends and family. Avoiding pain makes us feel safer in the moment, but it can lead to unproductive thoughts:

+ "I'm so depressed, I can't go out."

+ "I'm so fat, I can't date."

+ "I'm in so much pain, I'm just going to have another drink and forget about it."

Short-term, pain-driven thoughts often lead to impulsive actions that just make the problem worse. Inflexible thinking like this can lead to negative outcomes, such as addiction, loneliness, or increasing feelings of hopelessness and sadness.

Good mental health means psychological flexibility. It means that you might have to reconsider some of your beliefs that don't serve you. So, for example, if you value having a creative career, you might challenge your belief that you can only make enough money in finance or law. If you value a healthy romantic relationship, but your work requires international travel, you may have to challenge a belief that relationships work only when you and your partner are living together all the time.

At first, you might think, "without these rules, my life is going to fall apart." But the reality is quite different. Letting them go increases your ability to adapt and deal with change. This flexibility allows you to broaden your world and have new experiences. As you go through this book, allow yourself to try on some new behaviors and beliefs without judging them.

Remember: A better life is the by-product of adhering to your values and being flexible.

TAKEAWAY

✦ Everyone has an inner compass; grief can be a magnet masquerading as your true north.

✦ Assessing situations in the context of your values allows you to make healthy, conscious decisions, rather than defaulting to unproductive behaviors.

✦ Flipping the script on negative self-talk is a powerful tool for refocusing on the positive.

✦ Prioritizing your values leads to the greatest success.

✦ Increasing psychological flexibility leads to greater fulfillment.

✦ You don't need to "get over it" to have a better life.

CHAPTER 3

Following Your Inner Compass

The Big Idea: Committed Action

Identifying your core values is the first step toward moving your life into alignment with your values. Taking repeated committed action based on your values will help you increase your resilience, accept your loss, and move through your grief. Some of this action will be physical, for example, if you value improving your health. Some of it will be mental, as you prepare your mind for a new way of living, thinking, or behaving.

Persistence is going to be important here. You will inevitably find yourself facing obstacles. Some barriers may be obvious, such as having inadequate funds or lacking certain skills. Other obstacles will be more subtle, such as a partner or family member who is invested in keeping everything the same. Spend some time thinking about how you might work around your obstacles.

Sometimes you just need to keep moving, even when your grief is heavy. Perhaps your spouse has died, but you still value family, so you make a choice to play with your grandchildren regularly, even though you're sad. Or maybe you feel angry and discouraged, but one of your values is a rich creative life, so you make a commitment to practicing the piano regardless of how you feel. Your journal will help you, as will consulting with trusted friends or advisors. There are also some amazing support groups, listservs, and other resources on the web. One of my favorite places to find peer-to-peer support is on Facebook, which seems to have a group for everything. The site can also be a great place to post an accountability request or request for support like, "I'm committing right now to meditating for 20 minutes a day. If I don't post about it every day, please feel free to call me out on it."

Flexibility is key here; your values and actions need to be living, breathing parts of you. Trying to live by someone else's goals or values is likely to result in resentment, depression, and failure. When you encounter obstacles, difficult feelings are bound to crop up. The question is: When the going gets tough, can you keep your eye on what you stand to gain? Even when the goal seems impossible, you can always start by making mental shifts in the right direction.

By taking committed action, you will move through the process of untangling your thoughts and feelings—actions that allow you to move forward in the direction of your goals. Are your goals realistic? Try breaking them down, step-by-step, to identify potential trouble spots and start thinking about ways to get assistance with them. Maybe that means taking an extra job, rearranging your schedule, or making a public commitment.

Living your values is a lifelong journey. You won't be happy just because you met a goal, but you will notice a change as you move in alignment with your values. Taking committed action will often feel uncomfortable, precisely because it is out of the norm for you. But like most things, living your values becomes a habit the more you practice it.

TRY THIS: Bring Your Values to Life

Because the cost of behavioral avoidance (e.g., skipping activities, avoiding people, or numbing your feelings) is so high, we're going to get right to the work of bringing your values to life. You will need your journal again. Pick three behaviors that will move you closer to the number one value you identified in the last chapter. These behaviors form the basis of your committed actions. Here are some examples of how this approach works.

If your value is family, then your committed actions might be to

+ Go to the movies with your brother

+ Schedule a regular weekly phone call with your grandma

+ Cook a family dinner every Wednesday night so that you can all spend time together

If your value is improving your health, your committed actions might be to

+ Eat at least one fruit or vegetable at every meal

+ Walk for 20 minutes a day, five days a week

+ Make sure you get a solid eight hours of sleep per night

Commit to these actions, consistently, no matter what your grief tells you. If your grief says, "none of this matters, there's no point in getting out of bed," acknowledge your grief, but make the choice to get out of bed and take committed action. If your grief says, "eating an apple isn't going to fix your diabetes," again, acknowledge your grief as unhelpful, and choose the apple. Because the truth is that going to a movie with your brother or eating an apple instead of a pastry eventually will result in changes—a closer family or stronger body.

How Taking Committed Action Will Help

Taking committed action has many other benefits beyond helping you move through grief—benefits that will motivate you in a way that makes ongoing action-taking easier and easier. As old thinking habits and habitual but ineffective behaviors take up less space in your life, committed action brings you more into alignment with your values. Obtaining the benefits is not the goal; it just happens. The life you want is no longer one you're just thinking or dreaming about; it becomes a life that you're actually living. Your old thoughts and behaviors will have less power, which means you will spend less effort trying to push them away. The grief will feel much less intense too. But remember, that's not the goal here; the goal right now is just to keep moving.

Our minds have overlearned the habit of being anxious. We might be anxious about driving on the freeway, calling friends to make plans, presenting projects at work, or even just walking out the front door. We do anxiety really, really well. But when you learn that what you fear usually doesn't come to pass, your anxiety decreases. And when the thing you fear does happen, you'll often find that it doesn't matter as much as you thought it would. You learn how to live with the inevitable disappointment of life. As you take committed action, you'll discover that you're a whole lot more competent than you thought you were. In a good way, we're going to make a liar out of that persistent voice in your head—the one that says, "this will never work, you can't do this, you're not good enough . . ."

Figuring out workable actions will take some trial and error, but your skill for creating flexible behaviors will get more polished over time. As you accomplish some of your goals, you will develop a sense of pride in what you're doing and how you're changing. You will also have a new or renewed sense of competence when you see how effective your actions truly are.

This movement toward a new sense of self will probably seem slow, painful, and awkward at first. You may have a lot of judgments about how well or how poorly this new approach is working. For now, I'm going to ask you to make a conscious choice to suspend judgment and just keep taking action. Notice yourself taking the actions. Be curious about your internal responses to the actions and your thinking about the actions: "Isn't that interesting how I always get an upset stomach before I make a phone call, but when it's over five minutes later, I feel like I accomplished the most amazing thing?" "Why is it that I hate getting out of bed early and going outside to take my walk, but I feel so much better after the walk?" You are not actually separating from yourself; you are developing what we call the observer self, a valuable part of you.

The observer self is important because it is the part of you that is sensible and clear-headed. Rather than becoming overwhelmed by emotions or ineffective actions, the observer self sees the proof of a life well lived in the values that come to life through committed action. A sense of confidence builds when you activate this observer self—when you get curious about what's going on inside of you. It's much scarier to get trapped in the experience of having all of your thoughts and feelings hit hard and fast, without order or control, like they do so often when you're grieving. By taking a step back, you may start to see that what you thought was true is not necessarily true—an experience that can be quite freeing. In the process of this shift, you begin to experience a new vitality and zest for living.

Since values without action are meaningless, you need to act in a structured way. Here, we will create a list of workable actions that you can refer back to on a daily basis.

You'll need your journal or notebook. Write your top three values down the left side of the page. Beside each value, make a list of five committed actions for each of your three values. Leave yourself a little space on the right side of the page for rating each committed action, which is described below. There will be 15 actions total.

On the right side of the same page, rate how difficult it will be for you to take each action on a scale from 1 to 10, with 1 being the easiest and 10 being the most difficult. Use the same 1 to 10 scale to rank how likely it is that you will take the action.

Now, choose an action with a low difficulty score and a high likelihood score. Take this action within the next 24 hours. Stay focused on the value that you're moving toward at all times, especially if you're feeling doubtful about your ability to take the action.

Meeting Your Grief with Committed Action

Feelings like grief, hopelessness, and depression tell us that it's better to just sit still, be quiet, and do nothing. And, to be sure, making any kind of effort feels much too hard when you're grieving. It may feel overwhelming, or even completely incapacitating. This lack of motivation is one of the symptoms of depression, as well as grieving.

But the thing is, your painful thoughts and feelings are not telling you the truth. You might even call them fantasies. They're not fun fantasies, though. They're the kind of fantasies that make you feel worse—more hopeless and more stuck—leading to dark thoughts, catastrophizing, and more grief and loss. These thoughts are leading you away from joy, and deeper into your grief. These fantasies are giving you information, sure, but that information is just data you should consider, not reality that you must abide by.

Meeting your grief with committed action is the antidote to living in the quicksand of fantasies, false beliefs, and unproductive behaviors. You do this by starting small, with easier actions, and working your way up to bigger, more difficult actions. Each action you take gives you momentum, making it easier to take the next step. Every small bit of progress is like a brick in a wall. One or two bricks doesn't even make a pile, but 50, 60, or 70 bricks start to look like a meaningful wall. Similarly, one or two notes doesn't make a song, but many notes arranged intentionally do. They may even make an album.

Starting small is also a great way to stay in the mind-set of willingness. If you were to start with the biggest, most difficult action you could imagine ("I'm going to ask her to marry me" or "I'm going to quit my job tomorrow"), the likelihood of it happening is pretty small. Know that taking these actions is going to be awkward and a little painful, especially in the beginning. And it's work. But taking small steps gets you in the habit of doing the right thing for yourself, because even small steps are aligned with your vision and values. Small gains become larger and more meaningful over time, as they grow in alignment with your values.

The process of implementing goals and behaviors that are related to your values is both active and intentional. When you're paying attention, you're really living in the present moment, and things go better. Living in the past or the future will get you stuck in depression or anxiety. Many of the unproductive actions you've impulsively chosen in the past have led to undesirable consequences, haven't they? You believed your thoughts and ended up mired in anxiety, addiction, depression, and grief.

Everything gets worse when you impulsively avoid certain situations, or self-medicate, whether through substances or behaviors. Believing that your thoughts are true will make life difficult for you; such belief leaves you feeling like you've got no choice but to do what you've always done. As the famous saying goes: The definition of insanity is doing the same thing over and over and expecting different results. We are looking to move to a place of sanity, clarity, and peace. Choosing to live in accordance with your values, no matter what you're feeling in the moment, will lead you to a new place. In committing to taking values-based actions, you are increasing your resilience, speeding up your progress, and making space for joy, even while you're grieving.

DON'T PUT ON A HAPPY FACE

When you were a baby, you didn't hide your feelings. You cried when you were hungry or wet. You made a weird face when you were gassy. You smiled when someone smiled at you, and you giggled and cooed when you were content. But over time, through social conditioning, we learn to hide how we really feel.

In many ways, hiding our feelings is a useful tool. We all respond to the common greeting "How are you?" with a quick, automatic "Fine" or "Good; how about you?" Do you really want to engage in a deep conversation with your postal clerk, or the colleague you bump into in the bathroom? Probably not. You'd rather just get your package or finish your business. It's okay to be courteous, but not engaged.

The downside of this conditioning is that you stop sharing your true feelings. Many families only allow or model positive emotions. Directly or indirectly, you are told that it is not okay to talk about or experience anger, regret, sadness, jealousy, or shame, which in turn decreases your ability to detect or accept your feelings. You also miss out on the support and connection that comes from authentic engagement with others. People assume all is well, and they don't offer help. You end up feeling isolated and unsupported, especially at times when asking for help is hardest.

You are not required to put on a happy face when you're grieving; it's actually counterproductive to do so. Instead, take a risk and try telling the truth when someone asks how you're doing. Tell them you're still feeling sad, disoriented, or lonely. By speaking your truth, you are easing your path through grief.

You will need your journal for this exercise, which is about creating SMART goals. SMART goals are:

S = Specific/Simple

M = Measurable/Motivated by Values

A = Attainable/Action-Oriented

R = Realistic/Reachable

T = Timely/Time-Based

SMART goals enhance your skills by adding structure, which helps keep you motivated. You don't have to use them all the time, but they can be helpful when you feel like you need a specific plan. Just check back in with your SMART goals and see what to do next.

Say your goal falls under the value of "family" and is about "feeling closer to my kids." Here's how you might break it down:

S = Have a weekly family meal where electronic devices are banned.

M = Time spent together will lead to more connection.

A = One night per week, every week, is reasonable.

R = Very realistic.

T = Implement immediately and repeat weekly.

Another example might be that you want to develop a daily 20-minute meditation practice as part of your self-care and health value.

S = Download a free meditation app and do a five-minute guided meditation on Monday, Wednesday, and Friday.

M = Five minutes is a clearly defined measurement; three days per week is as well.

A = This action appears to be reasonable; it's only 15 minutes a week total.

R = Yes. No special tools or teachers are required.

T = You can start within 24 hours and adjust your goal to increase time and frequency.

You can create SMART goals around almost any part of your life. The smaller your actions, the more likely you are to take them and the greater your chance of success. All great achievements start with one small action; this is how you begin to create a values-rich life.

Moving Forward with Committed Action

Values help us determine what actions we will take next. We can begin by asking ourselves: "Will doing this move me closer to my values, or farther from them?" For example, "Will staying in bed and skipping this family outing take me closer to my values of family and community?" If the answer is no, then the thing to do is get out of bed and go, despite what your pain is telling you. Or, "Will eating this donut move me closer to my value of health and wellness?" If not, put the donut down.

Letting your grief or other feelings make decisions for you quickly leads to isolation, inactivity, and even greater feelings of sadness, anxiety, and shame. Forward movement is built into committed action, because committed action always moves you toward your goals, which move you closer to a life filled with what you value.

In order to keep moving toward your goals, you need to know that the brain can be a bit of a liar. Imagine a little gremlin sitting on your shoulder, poking and pulling at you. The gremlin will try to keep you stuck, or even suggest things that move you away from your goals ("try the cocaine," "don't pick up the phone when your mother calls," "you don't need to go to church"). It will tell you "you're not worth taking care of," "a little bit doesn't matter," and "no one will know anyway." But you are in control of the bigger, better part of your brain. Your brain can generate positive motivational messages too: "you're worth it," "you can do this," and "a tiny bit of effort will make all the difference." When you listen to this part of your brain, you keep moving toward your goals, because you know and believe that your actions will pay off in a good way.

Being purposeful in how you approach your goals and staying focused on your purpose requires daily commitment. Committed action is not something you do once for five minutes, dust off your hands, and then magically see the desired result. You need to keep gently returning your focus to your goals, several times a day. Be kind to yourself, but don't slack off. It's helpful to take a picture of the goals page from your journal so you have it with you at all times, or write a list of your goals and values on your phone. You can also keep your list in other places, like posted to your bathroom mirror or on your nightstand, so you can look at it when you wake up and again when you go to sleep.

Time is a critical factor in attaining your goals. When you say "maybe someday" or "I'll get around to it," what happens? If you're like most people, nothing happens. And when you are grieving a loss, it's even harder to get motivated. Add a discouragingly difficult list of tasks, and you're almost guaranteed to fail. That's why it is helpful to focus on setting time frames for your goals, as described in the SMART goals exercise above. Because these are your time frames, you can adjust the numbers and deadlines as needed. Starting with a reasonable goal means you will put some pressure on yourself in a good way.

Assessing your progress in a semiformal way by going through your list daily and checking off activities you have completed, as well as reviewing your overall accomplishments once a week, is also helpful in keeping you moving. When you're in the depths of your grief, it's hard to see progress. Crossing things off your list makes progress visible; it serves to cement the idea that you have taken a step forward.

TRY THIS: Old You, New You

Our brains get lazy when they're accustomed to acting in a certain way, even when the results are harmful. You need to figure out new ways of doing things, since it no longer works to default to the old ones (assuming the old ways ever did work). What you are are trying to do is think in a more psychologically flexible way—one that brings you peace and happiness.

Grab your journal and spend a few minutes answering the following questions from the perspective of the old you and the new you. Use the past tense when writing about the old you, and the present tense when writing about the new you, as I've done below:

Old You:

+ What were your favorite ways of handling problems (e.g., lying, manipulation, passivity, blaming, or avoidance)?

- How did others experience you when you used these methods?

- How were you living by your values when you were behaving in these ways?

New You:

- What are you doing now that you can't resort to your old ways of problem solving?

- What are some new values-aligned behaviors you are trying, or plan to try soon (e.g., assertive communication, positive self-talk, influencing others in a healthy direction, releasing control, or accepting limitations)?

- How are you living by your values as you try new behaviors?

Intentional change requires effort, knowledge, and commitment. Getting familiar with the unproductive behaviors and beliefs you hold strongly is essential to change. Let your values guide you, release the old way of thinking, try some new behaviors, and allow change to happen.

Allowing Change to Happen

Change requires giving yourself permission to change, the time and space to make changes based on solid information, and support for the process of change.

When you picked up this book, you started to give yourself permission to change. Something wasn't working. You were feeling overwhelmed by your loss, and you made a decision to seek help and change. There is no need to stay stuck in old thoughts or behaviors that don't work for you anymore.

Taking action in the face of grief can be very difficult. Sometimes you freeze up and can't think at all. Your willingness disappears along with the creative part of your brain that lets you formulate plans and goals. You may feel scared about what's going on in your family or the world.

For example, you might be painfully surprised to discover that there are a lot of things you don't know how to do, like look for a job after 20 years of employment, find a new partner in the online dating world, or manage your finances. Other monumental tasks, like clearing out the home of a deceased loved one or administering an estate, can weigh heavily. Or you have a whole new set of problems: a child who starts using drugs after his father dies, or a plummeting real estate market just when you need to sell a home.

All of these things may feel even more unmanageable when you're crying frequently, feeling lonely, and worrying about the future. It's natural to hunker down, be still, retreat, or just do nothing. However, that is not productive. Referring to your values and related list of actionable goals is going to get you through these difficult moments. You have defined your own values and goals—and, in the process, created a very reliable roadmap.

And still, some of these changes are going to take time (probably more time than you'd like). These changes may also need a little space to happen. When you're dealing with grief, change comes slower if you hold on tightly to the past. Hold lightly—which is to say, don't forget the past, or who or what you've lost, but don't cling to it like that's all there is.

Supporting yourself with planning, accountability, and loving redirection will get you far when it comes to taking committed actions on a regular basis. As your psychological flexibility and resilience increase, you can take bigger chances—giving yourself more choices and opening up more possibilities for yourself.

TAKEAWAYS

+ Your painful thoughts and feelings are just that; they are not the truth.

+ Committed action is the tool that transforms your values into lived experiences.

+ Prioritizing your values and goals makes them more achievable.

+ You don't need to put on a happy face.

+ Forward movement naturally evolves from actions that are aligned with your values.

+ You must choose to allow change to take place.

CHAPTER 4

Coming to Terms with Pain

The Big Idea: Acceptance

Acceptance is the pillar that steadies you as you move through difficult feelings. It helps anchor you during the grieving process. It is always there, strong and solid, bringing you back to center when you start to feel confused, distracted, or distressed. Acceptance is really a huge relief—it means recognizing what lies within your ability to control, and what is beyond your control. Acceptance means acknowledging both the manageable and the unmanageable parts of life. You can choose how to behave, but you cannot change the facts of your loss.

Most of us think acceptance means grudgingly dealing with something we don't want or don't like. Active acceptance is different. It means not:

+ Giving up

+ Giving in

- Surrendering
- Tolerating
- Failing
- Being defeated

The kind of acceptance we're talking about has to do with making active choices, consistently, without judgment. You might have hopes and expectations, but there are no guaranteed outcomes. Whether you achieve what you're hoping to achieve or not, you accept the result without declaring it good or bad. Think of it as something that broadens your experience, something that means you are:

- Opening up
- Allowing
- Leaning in
- Breathing into
- Creating space
- Expanding
- Being willing
- Releasing the struggle

You're not trying to change anything. You are making room and being present as your feelings come and go. Trying to get rid of your anxiety, grief, or depression only increases their intensity, as well as your suffering. The process is simple, but requires practice. In sum: Notice your unhelpful thoughts. Don't resist these thoughts; watch them pass.

Try thinking of it like this: Envision the floor of a stock exchange, with the board running a constant stream of data. Instead of numbers, though, your thoughts, feelings, perceptions, and experiences run across the board. The stream moves so fast, you don't have time to judge or react. You have to release information as it passes, because more information appears immediately. Allowing the release contributes to acceptance.

Although the steps are simple, you may struggle with them as you try to consciously achieve a state of acceptance. Some tools you might use to build acceptance include:

+ Noticing the feeling (Where do you feel it in your body? Does it have a color or sensation? A temperature or texture?)

+ Normalizing the feeling, as Russ Harris says, by reminding yourself that all humans have similar feelings, and that feelings may be painful when there's a gap between what you want and what you've got.

+ Naming the feeling mindfully ("Here's my anxiety again," or "Oh, that's the sadness").

+ Allowing the feeling to expand: Identify where you feel it in your body, imagine that it's a balloon you are blowing up, and see it get bigger and bigger until it fills your entire body. Notice that you are able to accept the feeling, despite it having gotten much larger.

The most important things about the practice of acceptance are to be gentle with yourself and to be curious.

Being gentle with yourself means recognizing that human beings are complicated creatures, grief is messy, and that you're doing something new—something that requires both willingness and repetition. Give yourself permission to do things "wrong." Being gentle with yourself also means taking time, asking for and accepting support, and crying as often as needed (this is where non-judgment is extra helpful).

Curiosity is one of my favorite tools—and it is a powerful one, too. It is the opposite of judging, limiting, or opting out. It is about slowing down, paying attention mindfully, and wondering what's happening right now, inside of you, with intense interest. When you get curious, you develop self-compassion, and it becomes even easier to release your judgments and harshness. Anytime you need a little nudge, just say to yourself, "I am curious . . ."

TRY THIS: Listen to What Your Sadness Is Telling You

When we resist our emotions, they tend to get stuck in our brains as well as our bodies, causing irritability, depression, and low energy. Feelings are there for a reason, and sometimes we have to ask them what they're trying to tell us. You can start by getting to know your feelings from the inside out, in a process of gentle inquiry. You will need your journal and some quiet time alone. Be curious, open, inviting, and non-judgmental as you answer the following questions, exploring what your sadness might be telling you:

+ What do you associate with sadness? Brainstorm a list of everything that comes to mind. Don't edit.

+ Where do you feel sadness in your body? How would you describe it? Is it tiny or huge, soft or hard, colorful or dark, hot or cold, transparent or solid? Is it a lifeless lump, or full of active energy? Does it have a name?

- How do you know that this is sadness? What symptoms or experiences tell you that it's sadness?

- Whose voices are telling you what sadness is? Your own? A parent? A religious figure? A therapist?

- What do you do with your sadness? Hide it? Express it? Ignore it?

- What else makes you feel sad?

If you feel comfortable, write a dialogue between you and your sadness. Ask your sadness directly what it has to tell you. You might ask your sadness:

- Why are you here again?

- Why are you such a pest?

- What do you want me to know?

- Am I treating you okay?

- Do you want me to do something different?

Allow yourself to receive this inner wisdom. You can use this general format with any feelings you are curious about.

How Accepting Your Grief Will Help

One thing psychologists have learned is that many of the unpleasant symptoms and feelings we struggle with are actually triggered or worsened by the things we do to try to suppress, eliminate, or avoid them. The negative thoughts are not the problem; what matters is how we respond to them. Giving up the idea that our thoughts and feelings are true is one of the most powerful things you can do for yourself.

It seems that the harder we try to run away from unpleasant thoughts and feelings, the stronger they become. It's important to understand how these thoughts and feelings become traps that leave us in "spin cycle"—that thing that happens when your mind just keeps going around and around on the same topics, at high speed, like a washing machine. When you're in that state, your mind is not your friend and is not going to help you. Nothing changes, and you end up feeling wrung out and drained.

The process of struggling against how we're feeling is called "experiential avoidance." And although it may provide momentary relief, avoiding our feelings leads to outcomes in the long run that are almost always bad. Experiential avoidance occurs when we try to escape or avoid the thoughts, feelings, and memories that make us sad or uncomfortable. This can look like withdrawing from social life or family activities, using substances to numb the pain, procrastinating, or not addressing important tasks. Avoiding vulnerability like this often results in disconnection from the people you care about. You might even lose relationships altogether because of avoidant behavior. When you reach this point, the struggle against your pain causes more problems than the pain itself. Willingly accepting your grief counters the urge to avoid the feelings associated with it.

Withdrawing from life and isolating yourself is a very common response to grief. You're hurting and you don't want to talk about it, fearing that explaining your grief will make you feel worse. You don't want anyone to tell you to get over it or try to cheer you up. You want to be in your misery, and you surrender control to it. You feel like you're going to need all of your energy to fight it. I'm not asking you to give up your grief, just to approach it differently. When you do take a different approach and really stay present in the moment, regardless of what's happening inside of you, you can begin to experience more vitality and engagement with life. You can feel more free—like you can finally breathe again.

When you're feeling your grief strongly, your head is probably full of negative self-talk:

+ "Why can't I get over this?"

+ "It's been too long."

+ "I can't cope."

+ "This is too much for me to handle."

+ "I'll never get over this."

You've been living with those thoughts for a long time. It takes time to learn new ways of thinking and being, so be patient with yourself. Doing this work is not going to immediately stop your old thoughts from popping up, but it is going to let you take a step back and gain some perspective.

The work of acceptance is the work of moving toward discomfort, rather than away from it. The work is not about being fearless, but about accepting fear and anxiety in the moment—making them more manageable than when you try to avoid them. I can pretty much guarantee that life is going to be full of awful, uncomfortable, and downright painful experiences, for all of us. You are not alone in this struggle, and it is not loving behavior to try to avoid a universal human experience. Besides, unwillingness doesn't work. Unwillingness leads to missing out on the life you want to be living. Unwillingness also means you miss out on valuable learning experiences—experiences that might actually help you get better at doing new things. Living in the present moment and fully embracing the experiences that life gives you—with gentleness and curiosity—is more rewarding than trying to dance around and away from life.

TRY THIS: **Work with Difficult Emotions**

So many of our emotions are difficult to deal with, especially things like shame, anger, and sadness. Breaking down these thoughts and feelings, giving them space, and then choosing to release them is a powerful life skill.

Have your journal nearby to use after this meditation exercise. Read through the meditation to familiarize yourself with it and check back as needed.

+ Start by sitting comfortably.

+ Check in with your body; are there parts of your body that are not comfortable? Adjust as needed. If you can't adjust your body to ease the discomfort, just take note of it.

+ Close your eyes (yes, you can peek at the instructions!) and allow your breath to continue in its natural rhythm. Be curious about your breath. Do you feel it?

+ Now, recall a recent memory—something small that caused you distress, like an argument or a memory of feeling embarrassed. Do not focus on your grief or loss right now, because that would likely be too painful to sit though.

+ Remember how you felt at the time. Do any other emotions or sensations come up? Fear? Sadness? Just notice them.

+ Imagine that this feeling is being met with a gentle rainstorm of compassion. All the tenderness, love, and kindness that you would give a small child is yours.

+ Now say goodbye to your memory. Wave it off, watching it move further and further away from you.

✦ Allow your mind to settle, and reflect on how you feel. What are the sensations in your body now?

✦ Open your eyes and take a few minutes to journal about the experience.

You might even record the meditation into your phone's voice notes, with 30-second pauses, and use it whenever you experience an uncomfortable emotion.

IF YOU START TO FEEL OVERWHELMED

Allowing yourself to experience difficult emotions can bring up painful feelings or memories—feelings or memories that can make you feel overwhelmed. Thankfully, there are ways to dial back those painful feelings. By shifting your attention, you break the pattern. Here are a few ways to do that:

1 Focus your eyes on what is right in front of you, and give that object your full attention. Breathe deeply. Sit quietly, breathing, until you feel calmer.

2 Move your awareness from the difficult emotion you're feeling to another aspect of your present experience, like your breath. Keep returning your focus to your breath.

3 Scan the room, naming 10 to 20 objects in your head or out loud (e.g., green rug, beige couch, ugly sculpture).

Meeting Your Grief with Acceptance

Meeting your grief with acceptance doesn't mean giving in to grief, or even liking it. It's perfectly all right to hate what happened and how you're feeling. But by simply acknowledging that grief is part of your life experience right now, and giving up the struggle against it, you free up emotional resources—resources you can use to get on with living according to your values. This can be a tricky concept to really get, so let's try thinking about it in different ways.

Have you ever taken a country road trip, with nothing but a car full of gas and a vague plan in mind? You start driving, maybe referring to a map or guidebook, and stop wherever you find an interesting monument or restaurant. Along the way, you may find some amazing treasures, like a roadside stand full of fresh peaches or a quirky folk art museum. You walk in the gardens and forests and swim in the streams. And sometimes, you land in a restaurant with food so bad they should be paying *you* to eat there. Maybe there's even a creepy motel, a bout of food poisoning, or a windy and narrow mountain road that leaves you queasy and grateful to be alive. You just take the experiences as they come; you accept that a random trip is going to have the good, the bad, and the ugly. You accept that you need to keep going until you have finished your trip, regardless of the quality of experiences. This is like the act of accepting grief; some of the process is surprisingly okay, some is not so great, and some is truly terrible, but you just keep going. Living with this duality is really the art of psychological flexibility.

Every experience or achievement worth having requires some work, as with this grief journey. If you and your friends want to compete in a triathlon with an ocean swim, you have to train. You'll endure grueling runs, sweaty bike rides, sunburns, cramps, fatigue, bad weather, shin splints, water in your ears, salt up your nose, and waves crashing over you. You'll also enjoy the sunshine, the breeze, the companionship, and your sense of accomplishment. But the weather, the physical pain, and the fatigue can be huge challenges. You won't like some of the experiences, and you won't want to feel all that pain in your body. Many times, you will want to give up. But the race itself is worthwhile, and a certain pride comes with finishing it. To get to the finish, you must first accept all of the bad, along with all of the potential (but not guaranteed) good stuff.

Both of these examples include what seems like a pretty clear promise of positive results: a refreshing journey or a shared challenge with friends. With grieving, the positive outcomes don't come to mind as readily. "Feeling less lousy" or "not wanting to die" sometimes seem like the best you can hope for. The positives might not be obvious or may take time to really develop. No one can say if you write in your grief journal for 20 minutes a day that you will be finished with your grief in 90 days. We all grieve differently. And although there are no promises and no time frames, there is a lot of evidence that the practice of choosing acceptance simply becomes acceptance over time.

In tai chi, after you learn the basic moves, you enter into two-person sparring practices, which include something called "Push Hands." This tai chi sequence teaches students how to generate and handle power with coordination and neutrality. In part, Push Hands is meant to deprogram your natural instinct of resisting with force and retrain you to yield to and redirect force instead. By absorbing the energy of a force upon you, you deflect the force and remain standing. What a beautiful metaphor for the act of acceptance in the grief process! At times, you can't imagine that life will ever be good again. You feel that your grief will knock you down and overpower you. Maybe the best you can hope for is relief of your misery, a little less suffering, or that life will only be unbearable sometimes, rather than all the time. But by accepting the force of the grief, you can internalize the power of it, take ownership of it, and redirect it as strength and endurance, or what we call resilience.

GRIEF HAS NO TIMETABLE

You might be experiencing pressure to get over your grief and start acting like your old self. Insensitive people, maybe even your own family members, are asking why you haven't moved on yet or when you will have closure, whatever that means. Cultural expectations and religious rituals or practices around death and loss may exert their own pressure on you. If it's time for the *jahrzeit* (the anniversary of a death in Judaism), is that when it's time to stop grieving? Or when you close out the estate? Get a new job or home to replace the one you lost? Get pregnant again after a miscarriage?

I always tell my clients that they are the experts on themselves. You are the only one who can determine how long this process is going to take. You need to define your values, take intentional action, and make space for your thoughts and feelings. There is no wrong way to grieve, but there are more and less effective ways. Taking an active approach leads to the best outcomes.

Anyone who tells you that there's any predictable timetable for grief (a year is common) is flat-out wrong. The process looks different for every person. Grieving can last a few hours or a lifetime. The process can be nonlinear, sometimes delayed or complicated by other life circumstances. If you have a series of losses that occur in close succession, you may feel numb, confused, or frozen. If the experience of losing what you lost is particularly painful because it was violent, unexpected, or changed multiple aspects of your life, the resulting grief can take longer to work through.

The process of thinking is normal and natural, as is thinking continuously. If you are conscious, not thinking is an almost impossible task. Many mindfulness practitioners refer to the "monkey mind," meaning your thoughts are like an energetic monkey leaping from branch to branch, up and down, all over the place. Even our dreams might be seen as a form of continuous thinking. If you don't know how to handle this mental activity effectively, you may label this a distraction, a failure, or even call yourself a bad mindfulness practitioner.

Fortunately, mindfulness offers us tools for addressing the preoccupied thinking involved in worry, anxiety, and depression. One of these tools is called noting and labeling. Noting and labeling can assist you in detaching from your thoughts by loosening your attachment to and identification with those thoughts. This deconstruction process decreases the intense hold that some thoughts have on you. In this way, noting and labeling creates a kind of mental breathing room.

While practicing mindfulness meditation, you will go about noting and labeling like this:

+ Decide how you will label your thoughts. "Thinking," "thought," "idea," "sound," "sensation," and similar words work best.

+ Sit comfortably in a quiet place and close your eyes.

+ Set a timer for five minutes.

+ Consciously clear your mind and bring your attention to your breath. Almost immediately, you will notice your mind populating with thoughts: "I'm cold. My left knee hurts. Is that the building settling, or are we having an earthquake? I wonder how long I've been doing this."

- As each thought pops up (and they will start popping up, as fast as popcorn kernels exploding), observe and label it: "Thinking, thought, sound . . ."

- Let the thoughts go as you label them.

- Keep returning your attention to your breath.

Moving Forward with Acceptance

You may have noticed that we have not been measuring your progress. This is deliberate. The achievement of your goals is not *the* goal. The goal is really to keep moving, always forward, with acceptance. Acceptance is more than being in the present moment, not judging what is happening, and not seeing what's happening as a failure. Acceptance is an ongoing practice that will bring you peace.

Like mindfulness, acceptance is something you practice over and over again. There is no specific goal to achieve; the art of accepting is the goal. And acceptance is a habit. Right now, the process is like learning to drive. Remember when you first got your learner's permit and set out for driving practice? You were acutely conscious of doing every single step correctly, from inspecting the mirrors and the tires to making sure that your seat belt was on. You checked, double-checked, and triple-checked your mirrors and your blind spots. You put your turn signal on early, and every time. You counted "one Mississippi, two Mississippi" in your head at every stop sign to make sure you paused for a full two seconds. And parallel parking was utterly terrifying. You probably studied a diagram, and then went to an empty parking lot to practice, over and over again. Now, driving is substantially an unconscious behavior (but, hopefully, still a mindful one).

Mindfulness, acceptance, and your values similarly require a lot of consciousness in the beginning. You might try to memorize the meditations. You might get frustrated easily, not necessarily feel at ease after you practice releasing judgment, and even have to check a written list of your own values. You're aware of each time you "fail" in your attempts to let go, be present, stop judging, and keep everything in line with your values. This really is a lot of work, but you're doing it. No one does it perfectly (because remember, we're human), and you can still make significant progress.

Every step you are taking—reading this book, doing the journaling exercises and meditations, taking different actions, letting go of unhelpful thoughts and beliefs—is leading you in the right direction, because you have chosen the direction. Instead of stopping to judge, wasting time or energy on avoidance, or falling backward into the habits that got you stuck in the first place, you're taking deliberate steps. Know that trying to get rid of your pain can be traumatic, which is harder to deal with than being sad. As long as you're not going backward, you are moving forward. You are not making things worse.

Even simply being present in the moment is actually forward movement. It sounds like sitting still, but being in the moment requires your full attention and consciousness. It's different than what you've been doing your entire life. Being present while also taking a step back mentally, seeing what else is really going on, is invigorating. It's when we're down in the muck, flailing around, trying to swim through mud, that everything seems dark, hopeless, confusing, and overwhelming. Pulling back allows you to see that there is chaos, confusion, and difficulty, but you are only in it for a moment.

TRY THIS: Build Your Willingness Muscle

If you want to build physical muscle, you have to lift weights regularly for a few weeks before you start to see your body reshaping. At first, it's just hard, exhausting, and painful. But over time, you see change. Your body adapts to the exercises, and lifting becomes part of a healthy routine—a routine that actually feels good. In the same way, you can build your willingness muscle by bringing awareness to your limiting thoughts and practicing acceptance as these thoughts appear.

1   Get your journal, and use the prompts below to generate a list of negative thoughts or stuck points. Leave a couple of blank lines after each one, so you have space for the second part of the exercise. Feel free to add to the list as more unproductive thoughts come to mind.

+   I don't like
+   I don't want to do
+   I'm angry about
+   I'm unwilling to
+   I don't need
+   I miss
+   I want
+   I'm really resisting

2   Now, go back to each item and change the thought into something that feels more accepting. Be creative. Use words that are positive, flexible, affirming, and gentle. Here are some examples:

+   I don't like feeling like this, and I am managing okay anyway.

- I'm angry about my mother dying, and I know that the pain isn't permanent.
- I want everything to be exactly the way it was before my loss, and I accept that I can't change what has already happened.

The practice of changing your language might be clumsy at first, but changing the words you use—countering the negatives with adaptive positives—will change the way you think. Like weight lifting, changing your language becomes easier the more you practice it.

Allowing Your Change to Happen

Allowing change to happen can feel threatening if you've developed well-practiced behaviors of blocking or avoiding change. You might also identify with some of your behaviors. Are you known as a rebel, a clown, or an avoider? Are you seen as worthless because your depression or anxiety has immobilized you? Maybe you even think of yourself as a loser, a victim, or a depressive personality? As unpleasant as those thoughts may be, changing them can be intimidating.

Resisting and refusing change is not only impossible, it's impractical, and it compounds your suffering. Haruki Murakami, in *What I Talk About When I Talk About Running,* says that "Pain is inevitable. Suffering is optional. Say you're running and you think, 'Man, this hurts, I can't take it anymore.' The 'hurt' part is an unavoidable reality, but whether or not you can stand anymore is up to the runner himself." Choosing suffering on top of the pain just compounds the pain.

Whether you try to combat what life has handed to you is your choice. Choosing resistance leads to difficult thoughts and uncomfortable emotions, which in turn leads to unproductive behaviors—behaviors that run counter to you living your best life.

Allowing change to happen means accepting life on life's terms. You know from experience that resistance adds suffering to pain. The practice of non-resistance is acceptance—saying yes to life, no matter what life delivers you.

Accepting that life is going to keep right on happening, whether you like it or not, is like spraying WD-40 onto a stuck door hinge. Like magic, the hinge begins to move freely, letting you open and close the door without a struggle. All it took was a little lubricant. Your willingness and acceptance is mental lube: It frees up the anger, the sadness, and even the unkindness that you are exhibiting toward yourself in your worst moments.

Allowing change to happen is a gift to yourself. It says, "I don't want to suffer. I don't want to hold on to what is not working anymore." And you know what? You don't deserve to suffer anymore. Truly, you have suffered enough. No one else is going to start this process for you; you're the only one who can choose to accept the pain and release the suffering.

TAKEAWAYS

+ Acceptance is not giving up or giving in.

+ Trying to avoid distressing feelings and thoughts actually makes them worse.

+ Mindfulness practices help you learn how to tolerate your difficult emotions.

+ Your curiosity is a powerful tool.

+ You can easily master several ways to tolerate your emotions if you feel overwhelmed.

+ Life will always bring you pain; you have a choice about how much you suffer.

CHAPTER 5

Showing Up for Your Life

The Big Idea: Being Present

Have you ever been driving on autopilot, to the point where you found yourself at home and could not actually remembering exiting the freeway? That's what it's like to not be present. Stuff keeps happening, and you haven't got a clue how, when, or where it happened.

Being present sounds so simple. After all, where else could you be? But there are so many ways we are not present in our own lives. When you're experiencing anxiety, you're living in the future, worrying about all the things that might happen. When you're feeling depressed, there's a good chance you're really living in the past, thinking about all the things that went wrong, how you could have done them better, and so on. Either way, you are not present. Sometimes it looks like you're present, but your mind is a thousand miles away.

What we mean by "being present" is really existing in the current moment. You are aware of your environment; you are smelling, seeing, hearing, and feeling things as they happen. You are curious about your experiences, and you allow them to unfold without judging them. If you're anxious, you notice your sweaty palms and elevated heart rate. If you're sad, you feel your grief and allow the tears to fall. If you're happy, you notice the way a smile makes your face stretch.

When you're being mindful, there's a lot of data to be absorbed from the environment. Your experiences are both internal and external, and often happening simultaneously. Internal experiences include your thoughts, feelings, moods, memories, daydreams, and unconscious bodily movements, such as your heartbeat or breath. External experiences include the sounds you hear, sensory experiences like the wind on your face, the pressure and warmth of a hug, and the taste of the foods you eat. These experiences may also include the information that comes pouring in all day long from the news, other people, or electronic devices. Different physical environments and expectations, like the need to tend to a baby, show up at a meeting, or write a paper for school, are all external experiences that you take in—that become part of your complex internal landscape. All of these things require your mindful presence. They can all become overwhelming if you are not containing them to the present moment.

Staying present can be incredibly hard, especially when so much of what shows up in the present moment is painful. This is especially true when you are grieving, not feeling well, troubled by competing priorities, distracted by other people's needs, feeling many strong emotions at the same time, lack the necessary resources to take care of things, or are even just hungry or tired.

TRY THIS: Say Hello to Your Body with Breath

This practice will help you be present, mindful, and non-judgmental in an easy way. Begin by making sure that you'll have a few minutes of quiet privacy. Sit comfortably on a chair, couch, or the floor. If you're wearing any tight clothing, loosen it. Now, close your eyes and work your way through your body like this:

In your mind, say "Hello, body." Notice if any emotions or sensations come up immediately from this greeting.

Now, say to yourself, "Hello, breath." Where do you notice your breath in your body? Maybe you've never greeted your body or your breath like this, and it feels a little strange. Allow it to feel strange, or even a little uncomfortable. Continue breathing at your normal, natural pace.

Continue working your way through your body, starting from the feet, bringing the breath into each body part as you greet it, and pausing a bit after each "hello."

"Hello feet," and allow your breath to fill your feet.

"Hello calves," and allow the breath to move up into your calves, and so on.

"Hello knees."

"Hello thighs."

"Hello butt."

"Hello stomach."

"Hello heart."

"Hello shoulders."

"Hello arms."

"Hello hands."

"Hello neck."

"Hello face."

"Hello body."

Note where you feel heavy or light, relaxed or tense. Continue breathing into any spots that feel uncomfortable. Allow the breath to settle into these spots with ease. If there is resistance, don't fight or force it. Just notice it.

Silently thank your breath and all of your body parts. When you feel ready, open your eyes.

How Being Present Will Help

Being present, rather than being caught up in the past or worrying about the future, can remind you that good things and good feelings are possible, even in the midst of pain. When you're deep into your pain, sometimes you will literally feel like it's difficult to breathe. That is a very uncomfortable feeling—one that can contribute to anxiety, or worry about the future.

It's true that what you choose to give your attention to grows. Endlessly reviewing the past certainly leads to more depressive feelings, just as worry about the future breeds anxiety. Allowing yourself to be in the present moment moves you away from your grief. It's not that you don't have the grief anymore, but you're not feeding it with your time and attention.

When you are forward-focused and worrying about what's going to happen, you're missing out on the potential joy and satisfaction of the present moment. In effect, you are robbing yourself of time you could simply be living.

Being present allows you to stay in contact with what's going on around you. As your life circumstances evolve, being present allows you to make wise choices about committed action. When you're just dialing it in at work, mindlessly executing tasks and thinking about watching television later, you're not being present. You are wishing for reality to be different than it is. In the process, you may miss valuable interactions with colleagues or your boss, and lose out on opportunities to move mindfully toward your goals of financial security or career progress. Worse, you might make mistakes because you're not paying attention—mistakes that can actually delay your progress.

At the same time, you don't want to be in the moment to the point of judgment. Judging your present experience is one way of detaching from it. If you're thinking "these cupcakes could have been decorated better," you might miss out on the flavor of red velvet. When you're thinking "I don't like the way it feels when we kiss," you're missing the most important part of the kiss—the connection. Or if your internal judge says "I could have done a better job on this speech," you may miss the audience's appreciation.

Any time you are judging the moment, rather than being in the moment, you are taking something away from your experience. And you are automatically disengaging from your feelings. You are not smelling the flowers, but judging whether they are well arranged. You might be judging the food in front of you purely on appearance and missing out on some wonderful tastes. Or you are so busy evaluating the person in front of you that you don't actually engage with them. Missing out on both positive and negative feelings flattens your experience of life—something common in people who are depressed. People struggling with depression often feel disconnected, not noticing or caring about much of anything. They might even think they don't deserve pleasure or happiness.

Truly being in contact with the present means that, for those moments, you are suspending judgment. You are not dwelling in the past or getting hung up on the uncertainties of the future. It is an opportunity to use your curiosity to fully observe what is happening in the moment. When you make contact with your experiences as they are happening, rather than worrying that you didn't say or do the right thing, you are present. When you suspend judgment and just have your experiences, you, in effect, take the "charge" out of your experiences. Things that seemed scary or anxiety-inducing before can be met with curiosity and neutrality. When you can say, "This is happening, and I know it will pass," or "I don't enjoy this experience, and it's okay that I'm having it right now," you are being mindfully present and non-judgmental. The relief this can bring, even if only briefly, will help draw you further out of your grief and back toward your life.

TRY THIS: Be Present in Daily Activities

Bringing awareness to everyday activities like washing the dishes, folding laundry, and eating is an excellent way to develop your mindfulness skills. Try not to bring stress to the present moment; just focus on what is in front of you.

Love it or hate it, we've all got to wash dishes. Rather than getting caught up in anticipating how annoying it's going to be, how much time it will take, or wondering if you'll ever get that stuck-on cheese off the pan, just wash the dishes. Pay attention to the sink filling and the scent of the dish soap and how it foams. Observe the stains, grease, crumbs, and grime coming off the dishes. Notice the patterns on your cups and plates, and the handles on your pots and pans. Feel what it's like to be engaged in the task.

Folding laundry mindfully is a good practice in struggling a bit and returning focus. Notice how you need to fold T-shirts to fit in a drawer, or fitted sheets so they stack neatly in a pile. Notice the scent of clean laundry, the warmth of a towel out of the dryer, the textures of the fabrics, and the colors in front of you.

Bonus practice: Taste—truly taste—your food mindfully. First, look at it carefully for a moment. Notice its presentation. Close your eyes and breathe in its scent. Take one bite with your eyes closed, mindfully noticing the temperature and flavors. With your eyes closed, focus on the food with all of your senses. Notice the textures: crunchy, crispy, slippery, chewy. Taste the nuances: salty, fatty, sweet, bitter, acidic. Chew slowly, focusing on the pleasure of eating your food.

Meeting Your Grief by Being Present

Your life is more than grief, even if that pain is a big part of it right now. The pain is understandable and expected. But your life is also about joy, hope, and pleasure, even if that's harder for you to experience at this moment. Meeting your sadness, fear, and hopelessness by being present strengthens your resilience. It can help you reengage with your life and keep moving forward.

The past and the future are both kind of slippery—like trying to grab clouds. But the present is solid; it has texture and substance—something you can attach yourself to securely. When you're in the present, you're really in it. It feels real because it is real.

Fear of painful feelings drives avoidance, whether you are mentally disconnecting, refusing to interact with others, or using substances to numb out. If you're not feeling, then you're trying to catch clouds—you're not in the present moment. Engaging with the present moment is an immediate counter to the desire to avoid feeling, and being present gets easier with practice.

Cultivating a non-judgmental stance toward the things you are experiencing can help you detach from their intensity in a healthy way. Your pain, your happiness, the thoughts of hopelessness, even the voice that says it's too soon to be laughing again—all of that can benefit from non-judgment. Our judgments about the thoughts and feelings we have, activities we engage in, and experiences we avoid actually contribute to our pain—to the lack of enjoyment we get from our lives.

Pain is something most of us avoid as much as possible. Burning your hand hurts; getting burned in a relationship hurts even more. Losing something or someone is also painful. And yet, how would you know joy, relief, pleasure, or satisfaction if not for knowing pain? Thoughts of hopelessness can feel scary and surprising. They may be intense, especially when your loss is fresh. You might even think about dying. Although it is difficult, it's important to stay in contact with these feelings, too. This is why staying present with what you're going through is so valuable; the complexity of your personal experience is what adds richness and value to your life.

Experiencing happiness or laughter after a loss often brings up conflicting feelings. You probably know you want to feel happy again, even while you are grieving. But you may feel disloyalty to the person or thing you lost, or fear that other people might think you're being disrespectful, faking your grief, or that it's not really as bad as you say it is. There is no need to minimize your real feelings or give up your memories. Acceptance doesn't require being any different than you actually feel. Accepting the duality of life, your mind, and your grief is one of your resilience skills.

THERE'S NO RIGHT WAY TO GRIEVE

The experience of grief is unique, personal, and quite often highly convoluted. It's not a straight path from A to B. It's not even a zigzag path, or one with regularly scheduled rest breaks. It's nonlinear, not bound by time, and may offer up a host of confusing feelings and experiences. The experience of grief can pop up at odd times, like when you feel a spark with someone new after losing your spouse, when you have a child and wish desperately for your mother to be there with you both, when you go through an illness and fear your own death, or when you find your job or financial security threatened. And grief has a way of sneaking up on you just when you think it's finally settled. So whatever your experience is, whatever point or place in time you feel you're at in your grief, just let it be. Don't judge your feelings, and don't try to change them. You're doing it "right."

Sadness, missing someone or something, or feeling overwhelmed or stuck are all common experiences in grieving, but everyone will respond to loss in their own way. Some people quickly make radical life changes like selling a home, moving to another state, or even getting married. They work through legal and financial logistics quickly. For them, the only way to get through it is to keep on moving. If you know from experience that jumping headlong into the grieving process is going to be best for you, then by all means, move quickly.

Other people need to allow their experience to unfold over time, taking extended leave from work or school, and lots of quiet time. They make decisions more slowly and thoughtfully, but eventually get through it.

Some people prefer to grieve in private, whereas others need public ceremonies, memorials, speeches, and memorial pages. It's all okay.

Willingness to merely observe your thoughts can loosen their grip on you. "Leaves on a Stream" is a classic exercise in letting go of your thoughts:

+ Visualize yourself sitting on a soft, mossy patch at the edge of a stream. The trees are thick and green, the light is clear and beautiful, and the only sounds you hear are the gurgles of the water as it flows.

+ Sit comfortably. Allow your breath to flow in and out of your body at its natural pace for a minute or two.

+ Notice the thoughts coming into your mind. Without judgment, take your first thought and imagine placing it on a leaf in the stream. Pause and watch it float away.

+ Give yourself 10 to 20 seconds before you place the next thought on a leaf and watch it float away.

+ If a thought on a leaf gets stuck, wait 10 to 20 seconds and see if it dislodges itself and floats down the stream. If it remains stuck, consciously choose to treat it as an opportunity for growth, and keep moving.

+ If a thought disappears and reappears, repeat the process of gently placing it on a leaf and allowing it to float downstream.

+ Continue placing your thoughts on leaves in the stream for 20 minutes, or until you feel complete.

- ✦ Open your eyes and consider your experience. Was it easy or difficult? Peaceful or stressful? Take time to appreciate the process of allowing thoughts to appear, and then letting them go.

- ✦ Congratulate yourself for having successfully completed this exercise, no matter how imperfect its completion may feel.

Moving Forward by Being Present

Life is lived in the here and now. New learning happens here, too. And although reflecting on the past to learn from it and looking forward so you can plan the future are both useful, you can only experience the present moment as it is happening. Noticing things as they occur, without judgment, is the practice of staying present. When you are doing this, you are making contact with life, whether it is sad, happy, or somewhere in between.

When you are truly present and responding to your immediate environment, you can never get stuck, because the environment is always changing—there's always something new and interesting to tend to. A big part of psychological flexibility is allowing yourself to change, too. Letting go of internalized rules ("I'm depressed, so I can't go out," or "It's only okay to go to sad movies, because laughter is not okay") allows you to relax your hold on the past, continuing your movement through life as it unfolds around you. In the process, your grief becomes more fluid and flexible.

It is easy to start noticing life in the present moment. You can make a decision to do so, or set an alarm as a reminder for you to bring your attention back to the present moment. What's hard is to continue being present. So many things pop up as distractions. Paying attention to things that you might have once labeled as distractions—your rumbling stomach, the pain in your neck, someone else talking, that weird smell coming from the next room—are actually ways of staying in the present moment. These are part of your experience. Thoughts about what happened last week, or what's happening in an hour, are the real distractions.

Developing and maintaining sensory contact with your world can help you be more present in your life. So instead of seeing things as distractions or irritants, use them to ground yourself in the present moment. Pay close attention to the quality of light coming through your window as it wakes you up. Don't turn away when you smell that strange smell; get curious about it. Instead of just grabbing your clothes and throwing them on quickly, take a moment to look at the colors and feel the textures of the fabrics. Eating your usual for breakfast? Pause for a few seconds to really taste the first few bites before gobbling it up as you run out the door. See if you feel more connected to your life when you take these small actions to notice and engage.

Managing your experience in a more flexible, fluid, and voluntary way—a way that allows space for all of the choices and options to appear and be considered—also undermines struggle and avoidance. When you notice what's happening in the moment, you are actively disassembling the hold that the past has on you. Being present feels vital and connected—the opposite of how you feel when you are practicing avoidance.

Through this practice of present-focus, you learn through experience that most of what is present is actually non-threatening. Some things just need to be experienced or observed, and you don't have to do anything in response. Over-planning or over-anticipating usually increases anxiety. If you get yourself worked up, thinking "everybody knows that public speaking is stressful; I'm going to be a nervous wreck," then you set yourself up for anxiety and failure. But if you maintain curiosity, thinking "I've never been on stage before; I wonder how it will be for me?" you open up space for your experience to be positive. The act of being present is the act of defusing the negative energy connected to our old beliefs and habits.

TRY THIS: Write a Letter to Your Loss

Writing a letter to your loss gives you space to explore your relationship with it and allows your grief to dissipate.

You will need your journal for this exercise. As always, make sure you are comfortable and have some private time to do this exercise without interruption. You can use the following format and prompts to start your letter:

Dear [who or what you lost]:

Since I lost you, so much has been different . . . [write about what has been different, good or bad].

I feel so much grief ever since . . . [the actual loss, or what led up to it].

I am saying goodbye now because . . . [What is pushing you to make progress? How is being stuck interfering with your life and living your values?].

Saying goodbye makes me feel . . . [describe your emotional state].

I remember when . . . [you can talk about positive and negative experiences].

The best thing you gave me . . . [could be a memory, an experience, or a thing].

You taught me . . . [what's the most valuable lesson?].

My most difficult memory is . . . [keep it real; this is just for you].

Something I want you to know . . . [What do you take from the experience or relationship? What do you cherish? What do you wish you could have done differently?].

I will always remember . . . [try to focus on what you want to take forward with you].

Sign off with something that feels appropriate to your loss, such as "love," "fondly," or "respectfully," and your name as you were known to that person or in that situation.

You might say "goodbye" as you run your letter through the shredder, bury it, tear it up, or burn it safely.

Allowing Your Change to Happen

In order to allow change to happen, you must know how you feel at the moment, as well as what you want in the future. You also need to give yourself permission to go for your goals, and to keep moving even when things aren't turning out quite the way you wanted them to. Life can be quite unpredictable, and that unpredictability can feel a little scary. But you survived loss, and you are working your way through grief—working your way forward in your life. Keep giving yourself permission to move forward, ignore anyone who tries to discourage you, and have your experiences as they occur.

Let what's going to happen, happen, however it's going to happen. You can do quite a bit to influence an experience by showing up on time, staying present, and noticing what you are feeling and experiencing. Try to limit judgment. Observe and let go of any pesky, unproductive thoughts that pop up along the way. Don't try to run from your experience.

Accepting the outcomes, good or bad, will help you learn that, even when life is difficult, you can be okay being present in the midst of the difficulty. You see and feel your resilience and psychological flexibility growing with each new experience. I once was in the midst of a personal crisis. A dear friend of mine had relapsed with alcohol abuse after a long period of sobriety, and she was doing dangerous and self-destructive things, like driving drunk and showing up at work with a hangover. I badly wanted to do everything in my power to save her—fly out of state to talk to her, call the authorities to do a wellness check on her, or just do anything to "make" her stop drinking so that she wouldn't end up in jail or fired or dead. But you can't control another human being like that, especially one who is committed to acting out an unhealthy behavior. A supportive friend told me something that helped me detach with compassion: "Don't be attached to the outcome." It's a good mantra for detachment. It doesn't mean that you stop caring; it means that you move forward, just like you are doing now. Just as you have to give other people permission to live their lives, mistakes and all, you have to give yourself permission to move forward. Your values and goals can support you in that process.

TAKEAWAYS

+ The more you practice being present, the easier it becomes.

+ When you are present, it is hard to get caught in anxiety or depression.

+ Give yourself permission to have all the experiences, good or bad.

+ Being non-judgmental increases your ability to respond flexibly to stress and loss.

+ Don't be attached to the outcome.

CHAPTER 6

You Are Bigger Than Your Sadness

The Big Idea: Cognitive Defusion and Self-as-Context

You are not your thoughts, and you are not your feelings. When it comes to grief, this means that you are not your loss. Although sometimes you might feel like you are "sadness personified," you aren't. Things can't literally be sad all the time, but viewing life through the lens of grief can turn into quite a large "thinking problem."

Thinking problems happen when you think "everything is terrible, life is so sad, and I'm never going to be happy." This way of thinking is problematic because it's not objective—and it's also not true. Cognitive defusion and self-as-context are concepts that will help approach these thinking problems in a calm, even manner.

"Cognitions" is just another name for your thoughts, and "defusion" is another word for separating from them. Thoughts are not reality—they're just one aspect of your experience. If you succeed at cognitive defusion—defusing from your thoughts and your story about who you are or what you deserve—then you can begin to experience yourself in a new way. You can begin to see yourself less as the movie of your life and more like the screen on which your life is playing—as the context, or home base, for your thoughts, feelings, and experiences.

Think of it this way: Imagine you are a container—a container that holds many things. The container itself is not the things that it holds. In the same way, you hold many bits and pieces, random thoughts and ideas, your own beliefs, and others' beliefs—but that doesn't mean you *are* those things. That's what it means to see self-as-context. The first step toward experiencing yourself as context is to defuse from your thoughts about yourself and your experiences—to see your thoughts as separate from yourself.

You might think of the idea of self-as-context in other, more familiar terms: the observing self, the silent self, or the part of you that notices. To put everything together, we'll now focus on how to effectively separate from your thoughts and become a skilled observer of those thoughts. Your mind can be kind of like a junk drawer—a big pile of electrical cords, converters, remotes, telephone wires, spare pieces that came with the television, and other electronic stuff that everyone has stashed away. You might hang on to all this junk out of fear, just in case you need that one special part someday. But the drawer is a mess, and none of the items in it are accessible, let alone usable, until you organize the drawer. You have to step back, untangle everything, sort the items out, and then examine each one carefully to determine what's what. When you slow down, you can see that you don't need the remote for the television that broke, you no longer have a landline so those wires are useless, and so on. You can get clear on what to trash, what to sell, and what to donate—but none of that is possible if you just throw up your hands and say, "this is an impossible mess!"

Cognitions are necessary components of your emotional experiences. You need words, ideas, and images to identify and describe what you're experiencing. Sometimes cognitions are helpful, and sometimes they're not. Cognitions are helpful if they can create a shorthand to connect with others, or they allow you to seek help by accurately describing what's going on in your life. But these thoughts can be unhelpful when they're too strong—when they overwhelm you to the point of confusion, emotional distress, or even collapse.

Your cognitions can interfere with effective, values-based living. To gain perspective, you need to step out of them. When you're feeling strongly emotional, this can be hard to do. The practice of defusion, or separating from your cognitions, is a way to gain clarity on whether or not your thoughts are useful to you. Being fused with your thoughts means that they dominate your behavior, choices, attention, and actions. With cognitive defusion, the goal is to allow your thoughts to influence, but not override, your values.

You learn how to experience a stable sense of self by noticing yourself noticing—by bringing deliberate awareness to what is happening within you. Within your own internal "safe space," you can examine your thoughts without outside interference. When you develop a calm and consistent viewpoint—when you learn to trust yourself and your ability to manage your thinking—accepting things that seem difficult becomes easier.

COGNITIVE DEFUSION

We are fused with our thoughts when we believe and act as though they are reality. If we let them, our thoughts, emotions, and stories can convince us that they are objectively true. Your grief may be telling you that you are unlovable, at fault, or "damaged goods," but these are only thoughts, not the truth—not reality. You can shift your perspective, saying to yourself, "I'm a person who is thinking that I am unlovable," or "I'm a person who is thinking that I am at fault." Our thoughts are just temporary internal states, and they will pass. The minute someone tells you how amazing you are, or you get a new job, or you heal from your illness, those old thoughts are disproven.

Cultivating defusion allows us to practice experiencing our thoughts and emotions more objectively. Rather than getting caught up with your thoughts and emotions as though they reflect external reality, you can use your curiosity to take the emotional charge out of them—to see them clearly. Your grief doesn't mean that it's the end of the world; it means that there's something else you haven't seen yet. Detaching from the idea that "if I think it, it must be true," you can see that your thoughts are not obstacles, threats, or orders to be obeyed. You can say: "I think _____, and I'm going to try _____ anyway." Taking chances on something new becomes easier when you stop fighting with your thoughts.

TRY THIS: Play a Private Game of Rhyming "Telephone"

We all know how to play the game "Telephone." Someone begins by whispering a word or phrase to the person next to them, who whispers it to the next person, and so on. As the word or phrase gets further from the starting point, it usually turns into something silly.

This is a great way to practice defusing your thoughts, too. You don't need a group to do this, just your notebook and some creativity.

Pick a few phrases to start with, such as "I'm sad," "I'm a miserable mess," and "I'm the best." You can add more of your own as you get into the exercise.

Now, play with rhymes (for extra fun, say it out loud, with attitude):

"I'm sad, bad, mad, glad, a cad, a dad . . ."

"I'm the best, a rest, a guest, a test, a fest . . ."

Notice how the original thought is quickly forgotten, and maybe you are even laughing. Are any of these thoughts true now?

SELF-AS-CONTEXT, OR "THE OBSERVING SELF"

Self-as-context, or "the observing self," is a way of describing where you stand in relation to your thoughts, emotions, and experiences. The goal is to become the observer of yourself, rather than the embodiment of your thoughts and feelings. Instead of saying "I've never been so happy; I must hold on to this forever," you notice that you are a person thinking about being happy. Rather than saying "My nerves are all tied up in knots," you notice that you are having worrisome thoughts and the physical symptoms of anxiety in your body. Without labeling these experiences as good or bad, you notice the thoughts and choose to let them pass.

Taking the perspective of a neutral, confident observer is a helpful way of relating to the content of your life. Once you have built up your cognitive flexibility, you will experience yourself, your thoughts, and your experiences quite differently. We know that life will continue to be filled with challenges great and small, but those challenges won't seem so daunting, fearful, or permanently damaging.

If you're on a dream beach vacation with someone you love, and you've got plans to go hiking, dancing, and spend hours every day visiting tourist sites, stubbing your toe hard might immediately fill you with fear, let alone physical pain. Your thoughts might automatically kick in with: "You're such an idiot. What a klutz. You planned and saved for this perfect vacation. Now it's all ruined. You probably broke your toe. Everyone is going to be mad at you." But once you see that you can move your toe easily even though it hurts, your observer self can say: "This could have been much worse. It hurts, but I can still get around in sandals instead of sneakers for a few days. We might have to wait a couple days to go hiking or dancing. It's going to be okay."

If it's something worse, like a fender bender, your thoughts go to: "This is such a hassle. I'm going to miss time from work. I don't even know how much my deductible is. I wonder if my insurance is going to go up." But as soon as you verify that the other people are safe, exchange information, and take a few pictures for the record, you might shift into your observing self, who thinks: "That could have been way worse; I'm glad no one was hurt. I know I just paid my insurance premium, and I might even be able to pay for this repair in cash. It's not that big a deal after all, even though it's inconvenient."

When you are living in your "observer self" frame of mind, the hard things don't stop happening, but you handle them more gracefully. You don't immediately absorb the pain because you don't automatically believe your first thoughts, the ones telling you "this is a disaster."

TRY THIS: Self-Observation

Practicing self-observation at different times of day will help you notice themes in your thoughts and feelings. Altogether, this exercise should take about 25 to 30 minutes. Since it's easy to lose track of this process, it's helpful to set an alarm on your phone to remind you to pause, especially in the beginning.

At three separate times of day (morning, midday, and evening), pause for five minutes, close your eyes, and notice what's going on inside of both your body and your brain. Make a few notes in your journal: What are you thinking? Feeling emotionally? Sensing? What does your body feel like? Is your environment intrusive? Do you have to take a break and go to your car or outside to get a practice in? How is this experience different from being at home?

After the third observation, spend five minutes meditating on your observations and another five minutes writing about the experience in your journal.

How Defusion and Self-as-Context Will Help

When we are fused with our thoughts, emotions, and stories about our experiences, we end up operating as what is called "the conceptualized self"—a sort of idea of ourselves that we believe to be real and true.

But this idea of self is a fantasy—something we made up for ourselves over time. We take random thoughts, memories of emotional experiences, observations about what has happened, things we read, stuff we hear at school or work, and so on, and we convince ourselves that the thoughts now running through our heads are actually facts. The sources of these ideas might be your parents, friends, colleagues, or even movies, books, or television shows. And just because you have a thought doesn't mean it's the truth.

When we operate in this fused mode, our psychological flexibility is restricted, and we end up behaving in unhelpful ways—ways that can even cause damage. This inflexibility may keep us from living according to our values, cause more psychological distress, or lead us to engage in self-harming behavior like overeating, not showing up to work, or isolating ourselves from friends and family. Rather than responding to what's actually happening through contact with the present moment, we are responding to our thoughts and feelings about what has happened in the past or what could happen in the future. We mistake our thoughts, feelings, and beliefs for ourselves.

If you're grieving, you may have thoughts like "I will never be happy again, never love again, and never have joyful experiences like that as long as I live" or "I am clearly a loser and a bad person because I lost my job, and I deserve to suffer." If you are faced with thoughts like that, what are you going to do? You're going to drop deeper and deeper into negative thinking, find evidence all around you that supports the idea that the world is a terrible place, and create experiences that prove to yourself, once and for all, that everything is terrible.

It's certainly true that grieving is hard and loss is sad. That doesn't mean any of your other thoughts are true, though. And responding as if they are is not going to help you move through your grief, love again, find a new job, or work on getting your health back. This is where we use the skills of cognitive defusion to pick apart the thoughts, frame them a little differently, question whether or not they're true, and perhaps even make fun of them, or ourselves, for being so dramatic.

When we defuse from our stories and begin to make contact with our lives in the present moment, we are free to take committed actions that align with our values, rather than get stuck responding to the stories that play on an endless loop in our minds. This process might mean going out on dates despite doubts about future happiness, searching for a new job, or starting a new hobby that disproves your personal incompetence theory.

The opposite of this tangled web of thoughts—each negative, mean-spirited, self-damaging thought generating another one that's even worse—is cognitive defusion and self-as-context. Living in your observing self offers clarity, peace of mind, and the ability to access a more objective, external truth. With practice, as you grow in your skills, you will also grow in confidence. The more you practice, the more that moving quickly into your calm, clear-thinking mode becomes your automatic behavior. You are more easily able to put troublesome thoughts aside or quickly question them and make consistent, carefully considered choices. This practice decreases the desire to detach, ruminate, numb, or avoid. Living in alignment with your values becomes easier, as does staying on top of the tasks associated with your goals.

TRY THIS: Turn Down the Volume

The thoughts in our heads—the ones we're firmly committed to believing are true—can be quite noisy and intrusive. The really loud ones can completely overwhelm us into fear, inaction, or even total paralysis. When you are grieving—when you're trying to figure out what happened and where to go from here—the voices may become even louder and more compelling.

If someone else were able to listen in on your mind, what would they hear? Waves, rhythmically lapping at the edge of a beach? Static, like an AM radio station as you're driving through the mountains? Some form of deconstructed orchestra, with all the instruments playing at the same time, and no conductor? A poet, a concert pianist, a guy from another country, and a crying child trying to talk over one another in their unique languages?

+ Take your notebook, and write down the self-talk, chatter, and looping thoughts and statements that are piled up inside your head.

+ Now, make sure you have some privacy, because you're going to say all of these things out loud, several times.

- In your biggest, loudest, strongest voice, read each statement out loud. Try on different tones: angry, direct, and blaming.

- Soften your voice to a normal tone and read all of the statements out loud again, with a more neutral tone.

- Now lower your voice to a whisper, and read the statements out loud again, in a gentle tone.

Spend a few minutes journaling about the experience. What was it like to use different tones and levels of volume? Did your words feel different as your voice changed? Do your thoughts feel less fused, or less absolutely true? Do you feel a bit more kindly toward yourself and your thoughts now? Can you see how words are just words, not facts?

Meeting Your Grief with Defusion

Human beings are born storytellers. We are wired to detect patterns in our experiences, and to learn from those patterns. We use stories to make sense of our experiences. We connect with others by sharing the meaning and understanding found in our stories. And the stories you have created about your grief are important stories.

But sometimes, in telling our stories over and over, whether in our heads or to others, we become wedded to the "facts" as we see them. Breaking free of the story seems impossible when you have told it often. And when others hear your story, and retell it, it seems to become even more true. "That poor woman: she lost her husband, and then her house, and all of her money. She's had such a tragic life. I don't think she'll ever recover." This story sounds pretty dire, and it fits the paradigm most of us believe (loss leads to more loss, it's always tragic, and the damage is permanent). Although this type of validation can seem compassionate, it actually serves to drive us deeper into our grief.

These ideas of self and the meaning of loss that you tell yourself about what has happened are important and powerful stories—and *they're just stories*. This is not said to invalidate your very real pain. Instead, you are invited to step into the observing self, see your stories for what they are, and be willing to let your stories evolve.

Learning to rewrite and retell your story helps you defuse from your pain, which is critical to moving forward in your life. And because the stories you tell yourself are not the truth, there is really nothing to cling to. You want to consider the "facts" in your thoughts and stories and respond based on how useful they are to you, not whether or not you believe they are true.

TRY THIS: **Flip the Story**

Tear a sheet of paper out of your journal for this exercise.

On one side, write out your story the way you would normally tell it. Write the story as if you were sitting with someone for the first time and want them to understand just how bad your grief was.

Now, flip the paper over and turn it upside down. Spend some time thinking about how you might tell your story differently, in a way that turns your experience into a positive story with a good or happy outcome.

For example, your first story is that you got laid off from your job, which led to financial insecurity, fights with your spouse, and fear about the future. Now, flip the story: You received unemployment, got really honest about what you wanted the future to look like, relocated to a more affordable house, and you're happier in the end, even if you have a bit less money.

Meeting Your Grief with Yourself-as-Context

There's an inherent conflict between the observing self and the part of you that holds on to the past. Memories and mementos connect us to the past, and we are scared to let them recede—afraid we might forget the faces or voices of those we love, for example. But you can't be fully present in the moment if your thoughts are focused on the past.

The stories we create about what we have valued and lost hold us back. We start creating these stories when we hold on to something that we are losing or have lost, as we attempt to make sense of difficult experiences. The stories comfort us and may give us satisfaction. But telling new stories that focus on different elements of your experience connects you with the present, moving your grief forward in the process. As you think through a different way to tell the story, your experience transforms and becomes less painful. You are no longer in the story, but the observer of the story, just as you are the observer of your inner self.

Activating your curiosity can begin transforming the story. Ask yourself: What is my story? Is it true? Where did my story come from? Do I need to continue believing it? Is believing the story doing me any good? Use your psychological flexibility to assess your story. If the story is helpful to you, use it; if not, let it go like a helium balloon. You might be upset for a moment, but eventually the balloon drifts out of sight and you have to say goodbye to it. You can then choose to rewrite and retell your story until it loses some of its power to distress you. In the present moment, understand that your story is just words and pictures, not the truth of your existence.

If you've ever watched a crime show, you've seen a dramatic confrontation in the courtroom. One lawyer presents a case and his rock-solid witness. Then another lawyer conducts a cross-examination—one that could make even the most trustworthy witness look like a bigger criminal than the person on trial.

What are your beliefs about your loss—the thoughts you are certain must be true? Here's an example:

> **Belief:** If I'd gotten home earlier, I could have saved her life.
>
> **Cross-examination:** How do you know this is true? Do you have facts to prove it? Drawings of the home? What does the location have to do with her death? Isn't it true that she was 94 years old and had a heart condition? She was under medical care at the time of her death, correct? And she had a caregiver with her at the time of her passing?

Go through this process with the rest of your beliefs, dismantling the "truth."

WHEN "IT'S FOR THE BEST" ISN'T TRUE

The phrase "it's for the best," or something similar, is one you hear often when you're grieving. If you've lost a loved one, someone will say that it was better than them being in pain, or it's good that they finally went to heaven. If you lost a marriage, people will note that the marriage was difficult anyway and getting a second chance at love can be a blessing in disguise. Even if you've lost something like your health, someone will almost inevitably suggest that you have to look at the bright side, because now you can take charge of your health, and that's got to be so much better for you in the long run.

But just like your own thoughts, other people's thoughts and beliefs are not necessarily true. Most people are well-intentioned, and they're trying to make you feel better. It's good to be open to hearing other people's thoughts, but it's even better to consider whether those thoughts are true or helpful. Like your own thoughts and beliefs, you can choose to accept others' thoughts as your own guiding principles, or you can return to your values as a way to guide your beliefs and behaviors.

When people try to comfort you with their thoughts, test those thoughts against what you know to be true in the present moment. Use present-centeredness, and your observing self, to gain a little distance. Maybe you disagree strongly with what someone said. Maybe when a friend says "they're in a better place," what you really want is for that person to be in the best place of all—alive and right there with you. Even so, test the thoughts of others with non-judgment; it's okay for other people to hold their own beliefs, just as you hold yours.

Moving Forward into Your Life

A major loss can change so much, and when it happens quickly, it can feel like your whole world has flipped upside down. Our relationships, money, health, and possessions are indeed precious, yet it is also true that we must release some of what we've lost in order to move forward. Using the techniques outlined in this book so far, you have started to develop a practice of living in the present moment. Until you have practiced being in the observing self enough to know that it's usually a pretty calm place, it may be a difficult choice sometimes. Living in the present takes courage, as does stepping into your observing self to gain a little distance from your own experiences.

When you are operating from the point of view of the observing self, or self-as-context, accepting reality—good, bad, or neutral—becomes a new habit. Acceptance decreases your paralyzing anxiety about the future—it takes some of the charge out. Staying present with and attached to your anxiety in the moment can help you feel energized and motivated to deal with what's happening in life, whether that's work, life, family, or other relationships. When you stay present instead of projecting bad outcomes, challenges feel exhilarating rather than scary. In this way, a kind of "good anxiety" helps drive the actions needed to complete your goals. When you spend less time and energy struggling with anxiety, you can devote more attention to meeting the goals that matter to you—the ones that are aligned with your values.

Defining your values is an ongoing action. There might be an infinite number of values in the universe, but your core set of values is probably going to remain pretty consistent over the years. For example, if you loved school and learning, you're probably going to be a lifelong learner. Attending classes, reading books, and expanding your base of knowledge will be your consistent behaviors, because they are core values. If you value family, what "family" means will change over time from the family you were born into, the family you create yourself, and perhaps some other family of friends or spiritual community that evolves over time. Your specific actions and goals will change as well, in order to keep you moving in the right direction.

Redefining the life you thought you were going to have doesn't mean that you're letting go of the pain or the memories; it means that you're allowing the pain to come when it comes, then letting it pass as you observe it with curiosity and without judgment. The judgments we've absorbed from other people and institutions over time tend to be the ones that make us feel bad, guilty, wrong, ashamed, or useless. Releasing those judgments frees you to have your own opinions and make your own decisions, based on what matters to you.

You may also have to reconsider some of your values or goals. If you're a young widow who wants children, your values about family remain the same, but your partner will change. If you wanted to start a new career, but discovered that there was an age limit or health requirements you couldn't meet, then you may have to consider options that allow you to stick to your values (such as being of service, earning a lot of money, or doing something creative) with a different job title, location, or level of intensity.

Committing to trying new behaviors likely means investing in other relationships, which is a good thing. Healthy, active, honest, and engaged relationships almost always make us feel better, more useful, and happier with our life choices. You cannot replace someone you lost, but you can develop new friendships, communities, and romances that will help you feel fulfilled and satisfied with your life.

This type of self-care is a continuous process, not a one-time action. Trying out these new behaviors also is an act of self-care. The entire process of choosing to move forward, despite fears, obstacles, and unknowns, is in itself a tremendous act of self-care. The choices are all yours.

TRY THIS: **Write a Letter to Your Old Self**

Writing a letter to yourself can be a powerful tool for gaining clarity, forgiving yourself or others, confronting outstanding issues about your loss, healing some of the pain of your past, and gaining peace.

You'll need your notebook and a few minutes to write a farewell letter to the person you were, pre-loss. Use the second person (instead of saying "I," use "you," as if you were talking to someone else) to gain some detachment.

If your loss occurred a long time ago, write the letter to the person you were back then.

Be honest as you write the letter, and keep your tone compassionate and empathetic, writing as kindly as you would to a dear friend who has had a recent loss. Feel free to praise yourself for how you have been handling things, and say what you wish someone else would have said to you.

You can include helpful advice and suggestions for the future if you'd like.

Here are some prompts to help you get started:

You were such a [little girl, overwhelmed dad, or whomever you were at that time . . .].

Your relationships were so [tough, rewarding, complicated . . .].

There was so much going on with _____, _____, and _____.

You really handled it [well, with grace, as best you could . . .].

You've changed so much since then [describe the ways].

You've become . . .

I'm so proud of you for . . .

I wonder what the future holds for you [take a few minutes to imagine what is possible now].

When you've finished writing the letter, write a bit more about how you were feeling before you started writing, what the letter revealed about your values and goals, if anything surprising emerged, and how you feel now that you have finished.

Allowing Your Change to Happen

Peace, freedom, relief, and less sadness is what most of us ultimately want, of course, but giving up our current thoughts or beliefs about grief can also be its own kind of loss. In the normal evolution of life, when we are being truly flexible and allowing our life experiences to unfold without resisting, losses accumulate. Loss is part of the flow of life, and we accept it.

Deep grieving keeps us close to the person or thing that we've lost, keeping our loss very present in our immediate experience. We often compare every new experience to the old experience. Eventually though, grief begins to recede. The comparing and wishing that things were other than they actually are becomes less frequent and less intense. But people who have already experienced a major loss may be reluctant to invite another loss, and they may create internal roadblocks to moving forward. "I can't," "it's not possible," and "I don't want to" are phrases that indicate you may be acting out of fear about experiencing more loss, and unconsciously slowing yourself down.

Choosing to actively move through grief tends to bring us in contact with some of the most immediate, intense pain again. The layers of loss run deep. Grief moving through your body may even feel like a visceral experience. The sharpness of your pain may feel as bad as it did the moment your loss occurred, but the pain will dissipate over time as your thoughts and feelings move into more long-term memories. The sound of your partner's voice fades, and you can't quite recall it anymore. Eventually, it may be hard to remember other details about them. One year into cancer treatment, you no longer remember what it feels like not to feel sick. After years of unemployment, the routine of going to work every day is completely unfamiliar. You forget a little bit of who you were as you move forward through your grief.

Releasing those experiences can feel difficult, especially when we fear more loss, activating the pain, and we are uncertain whether we trust the releasing process. Giving yourself permission to move through the loss, the thoughts, and the associated feelings will help you move in the direction of your values. Leaving old ideas of yourself behind, and perhaps a certain lifestyle or daily experiences, are losses, too. But for every loss a new opportunity emerges along with a new way of being and experiencing the world around us—a world that may even be better than how we previously experienced life and loss.

TAKEAWAYS

+ Cognitive defusion is an effective tool for managing and detaching from your stress and anxiety.

+ "The observing self," or self-as-context, helps you gain perspective on your life when it feels overwhelming.

+ Fearing more loss as you let go of your old self is normal.

+ Writing a letter to who you were at the time of your loss increases your self-compassion.

+ Choosing to move forward with your life means that you will lose some details, but not the entire memory of who or what you lost.

CHAPTER 7

Your Path Forward

When you first picked up this book, you were feeling overwhelmed by your loss and having trouble coping with your grief. You were feeling sad most of the time and perhaps even had dropped fully into a period of depression. It was hard to make decisions about today, let alone the future. And you had some ideas about grief and loss that you believed quite strongly, though they weren't necessarily true.

Now, you have learned how to step back and look at your thoughts from a distance through your observing self, evaluating them with more accuracy in the process. You have learned to separate out thoughts that are useful, and set the less useful beliefs aside, all while checking and aligning your actions with your values, beliefs, and goals.

Rather than trying to eradicate grief and loss from our lives, we learn to live with them. There is no getting past grief or getting over it, and that's okay. Grief, like all of our strong emotions (anger, sadness, anxiety), is something that we must experience if we are to be fully emotionally engaged with other people and experiences, and present in our lives. Grief gets woven into the fabric of your life—it may soften in intensity, or fade over time, but it will always be part of your experience. Loss does not define who you are, but rather is an important element of who you are becoming. Grief informs your choices, but does not dictate them.

Your Life Today

Whatever your loss, it is something that you will carry with you always. You already know this on some level, but it may have been hard to accept—you wanted to get rid of the experience so you could get rid of the pain. It's understandable that you rejected the pain. You didn't have the best tools to deal with it. Now, you have learned to move through the many forms and phases of grief and to live more harmoniously with it. You've learned quite a few methods that are helpful for living this way, and you have started developing your resilience capabilities.

Hopefully, after working through this book and using the practices with some consistency, you have begun to notice a difference in how you are experiencing and responding to your pain. Perhaps you didn't notice your pain before because you were so adept at pushing it aside to try to limit your sadness, fear, or anxiety. Or you noticed the pain, but you covered it up quickly by faking happiness or numbing it with drugs or alcohol, so that you weren't even sure what it felt like anymore. Engaging with your pain is the harder choice at first, but also a much more rewarding one. Having surrendered to the idea that you can't control a lot of life, you are now more skilled at the practice of acceptance and you trust yourself more.

Your sense of resilience and psychological flexibility should be greater than they were when you started the practices in this book. You should have less fear and anxiety about the possibility of experiencing strong emotions, especially grief. And you should be more fully engaged with your life's enriching experiences and more in touch with what you truly value. You should be able to fully engage with whatever life presents you in the moment, good or bad, and view all of your experiences along a continuum.

But progress is never truly linear, particularly when it comes to grief. There will be ups and downs and setbacks. Some of these obstacles may be quite intense in the moment. You shouldn't interpret this as a sign of failure; it's normal and even desirable. Setbacks allow you to tap into your creativity and try out different possibilities—possibilities beyond what you had previously imagined or "known" to be true—which enhances your growth and psychological flexibility. Setbacks also allow you to experience yourself as more capable of handling challenges. Making a plan to carry such accomplishments into the future will help you sustain the strength and skills that you've gained.

Your Growth So Far

Evaluating and acknowledging your growth so far, while also creating a plan to continue growing, is an important part of the process of moving through your grief. Although we can't objectively measure your success at implementing this program, we can look at the factors that have shifted while you've been working through this book. If you look back at how you were thinking a little while ago, you will see that you have changed. You are the same person, with a different lens on your life and experiences.

Acknowledging your success is the embodiment of mindfulness—you are pausing in this moment and taking a clear-sighted look at your successes, remaining stuck points, and opportunities for future growth. Before jumping into planning for the future, acknowledge the hard work you've done so far. You have taken yourself from a place of fear and inactivity and moved into conscious, deliberate awareness. You've allowed your curiosity to awaken and have begun to see and experience your life differently.

Along with evaluating the past and acknowledging successes, focus on making a plan for the future. In the memorable words of Yogi Berra, "If you don't know where you're going, you might wind up somewhere else." With focus and intention, you will go on creating a rich, meaningful, and purposeful life. Repetitive engagement with the concepts and processes of values, acceptance, practice, and resilience-building can lead to a positive and natural outcome—improved psychological flexibility within the context of your chosen life.

Active and intentional choices lead to a satisfying, values-rich life. Making such choices starts with adopting the attitude that you actually do have choices—that life is not just happening at you, to you, or in spite of you. When you adopt a solution-oriented mind-set and finish what you start, you get better, more predictable results. Knowing how to apply the process of change consciously will help you achieve the things that matter to you. Accepting that moving through your grief is an evolving practice will help you maintain the kind of mental flexibility that will keep you moving forward.

When you start making changes, your optimism and ability to cope with difficult situations become personal superpowers. You now know from experience that you can increase your psychological flexibility. It's exciting to know that, even if you've been struggling for years, it doesn't take forever to feel the positive effects of new beliefs and behaviors. You are more self-confident and aware of your own strengths, so you see difficult situations as opportunities to become even more capable.

By identifying personally meaningful values, you have created reliable guideposts for developing the life you want, and you trust that the process is happening. You have a good sense of where you're headed in life and are actively involved in changing and developing your skills and circumstances to create a better life. You thoughtfully consider other people's values when choosing whether to follow through on their guidance or not. And you know how to use your values to create goals that you want to implement. Following this practice helps you create a solid plan for taking charge of your life, and you choose to do so, greeting life with an attitude of non-judgment, because it's easier and works better.

In the process of living by your values, you are also practicing living in the present moment. When you stay present in your life, you will find yourself noticing reasons for joy, even in the midst of pain. A growing sense of strength that comes from being present in your life means that you can always think of ways to make things better. There comes a certain flexibility in how you approach everything, and your goals become easier to readjust as the circumstances of your life change.

Having a life of your choosing is not a selfish act; it is an act of self-care and respect for yourself and others. This life is acting responsibly about your own health, as well as the well-being of others. Choosing to be around people you respect, who also support you, is also a way of taking care of yourself. You share your feelings with others and know when and where to get help. Because you are engaged with your life, satisfied with your choices, and have a clear direction, you are more resilient, more competent, more successful, and you persevere even when you feel challenged. This is a powerful measure of your success.

Begin to make your ideas actionable by putting them in writing. Take a sheet of paper and your list of values and set it up like the following example:

Value:

Long-Term Goal:

Short-Term Goals:

1

2

3

Long-Term Goal:

Short-Term Goals:

1

2

3

Long-Term Goal:

Short-Term Goals:

1

2

3

In this example, the value is about developing stronger, healthier relationships.

Value: RELATIONSHIPS

Long-Term Goal: STRENGTHEN FAMILY RELATIONSHIPS

Short-Term Goals:

1. Call my parents Sunday night at 5:00 p.m. and talk to them for half an hour.

2. Invite each kid for parent/child "special time" and work with them to create something fun and age appropriate.

3. Take turns researching and scheduling a date night with my partner once a month.

Long-Term Goal: DEVELOP NEW FRIENDSHIPS &

NURTURE OLD ONES

Short-Term Goals:

1. Sign up for Meetup.com under two or three special interest categories and commit to going to at least one event per month.

2. Every time I hang out with my old friends, put the next date on the calendar before we part ways. Don't just wait for it to happen.

3. Text my best friend or someone I'd like to know a little better every day; it only takes a minute and it's a great way to connect.

Long-Term Goal: ENHANCE WORKING RELATIONSHIPS

Short-Term Goals:

1 Invite one new colleague a week to have coffee.

2 Once a month, host a brown bag lunch and invite everyone in a different division.

3 Publicize a no-host cocktail hour at a neighborhood restaurant each quarter.

Keep this work handy, as you'll be referring to it for the next "Try This" exercise.

SELF-CARE WHILE GRIEVING

Grieving is hard work and takes a lot of energy. It's easy to forget the basics, such as eating properly, getting enough sleep, and staying hydrated. When you're grieving, remind yourself every day to practice self-care. If you need help, enlist a friend to remind you of the basics or do them with you.

+ Stick with moderate quantities of lighter, healthier foods (think roasted chicken rather than a casserole, or turkey sandwiches instead of burgers). Eat some produce at every meal.

+ Get seven to nine hours of sleep per night. It's okay to go to bed early so that you get enough rest.

+ Stay hydrated. Get half your body weight in ounces of water every day. If you weigh 160 pounds, for example, that would be 80 ounces, or 10 glasses.

+ Go easy on alcohol and caffeine. Alcohol increases feelings of depression, and caffeine can kick up anxiety.

+ Skip the drugs and cigarettes.

+ Get some sunshine and exercise—20 to 30 minutes a day is a good goal.

+ Try meditation.

+ Be kind to yourself.

+ Practice saying no more often.

+ Schedule more time with friends.

+ Get a checkup at the doctor and see the dentist.

Finding What Works for You

A plan for moving through grief might be the most amazing thing in the world, but it's utterly useless if you don't follow the plan regularly. I'm not suggesting that you need to love the plan—just that you find it tolerable and manageable enough to keep going so that you can get all the benefits. It would be difficult to create a program that is precisely aligned with your own natural rhythms, style, and pace, which is why it's important for you to claim this process as your own and modify it to fit your needs.

In order to do that, let's take a look at what has been most helpful for you about this program, as well as what didn't work so well. Once you've figured that out, you can tweak the exercises and suggestions to suit your own personal style so that you will keep working through them. Consider the following questions as you think about how you want to continue moving forward:

1 Which tools and strategies did you find most helpful? Did you enjoy the journaling exercises or struggle with putting your thoughts into writing? Were you anxious that someone might find and read your journal? Did that stop you from using it? Did the journaling prompts lead you into more freeform writing?

2 What about the meditations? Were they familiar and easy, a new challenge, or just a little weird to try out? Did you notice yourself getting relaxed as you tried them, or were you worried about doing them wrong?

3 Which strategies did you find the most challenging? Do you know why they were hard? Did you gain new insight from them anyway, or skip them? If something felt awkward, did you consider continuing to practice the strategy anyway, knowing that it would be beneficial?

4 What gave you the most insight about what you've been struggling with?

5 Would it be helpful to re-read some of the chapters now that you've worked your way through the whole book?

6 How often did you use the book—daily? Weekly? Intermittently? Did that feel like enough? Did you ever feel overwhelmed while making your way through the book, as though it were too much? If you felt overwhelmed, was the overwhelm emotional or was it logistical, like you just didn't have enough time? If 20 minutes of meditation is too much, can you handle five? If writing a short-term plan for all of your values is overwhelming, can you work on one value per day until you're finished with all them?

Perhaps you need to switch to a computer from handwriting, or vice versa, for the journaling exercises. Or you may want to record the meditations into the voice notes on your phone, so you don't get stressed out by bouncing back and forth between the content of the book and the actual meditation. It could be helpful to try out a few meditation apps that will help you continue your practice.

Or maybe you need to join a writing group or meditation center, which offer some built-in accountability, especially if there's a fee for participation or a consistently scheduled meeting time. Enlisting support from friends who are working on similar goals (your writing time might be a journaling exercise, while your friend is working on the first draft of a novel) can also be helpful. Finding a group of like-minded people who are working toward the same values or goals, such as creating better health (e.g., cooking classes, a walking group, or tai chi in the park), developing creativity (e.g., learning an instrument, joining a choir, practicing photography or dance, rehearsing a play, or painting), or growing their careers (e.g., creating portfolio projects for work, taking a computer programming class, or attending a networking event) will help keep you moving forward, too.

If "I'll focus on this later, when I have more time" is your mantra, and you've been reading along but skipping the exercises, try writing your values and goals on a paper calendar or Post-It notes, or program reminders into your phone. Schedule each exercise in by name, so that the reminders that pop up on your calendar aren't confusing. Brain fog, sluggishness, and forgetfulness are natural parts of the grieving process, so these things are not crutches; they're ways of ensuring that you give yourself the care and support that you need.

TRY THIS: Schedule Goals to Keep You Moving Forward

Although we are practicing being present-oriented, we also need to plan for the future in order to be successful at moving forward. Otherwise, there's a potential Groundhog Day–style trap of just repeating the same routine that leaves you stuck in grief.

To begin this exercise, use the worksheet you prepared in the last "Try This" exercise.

A system of calendaring your values-based goals will help you stay on track, even when you're feeling unmotivated. Try planning as much as a month into the future, broken down week by week. Here are a few examples of what this might look like:

Value: RELATIONSHIPS

(Write this on the top of a month-in-view calendar page to keep you focused on your value. If you don't usually use a paper calendar, you can download one from the internet, or just draw one on a piece of paper.)

Long-Term Goal: STRENGTHEN FAMILY RELATIONSHIPS

(Write this on the left side of your month-in-view calendar page to keep you focused on your larger goal.)

Now, decide when you're going to implement each of the sub-goals you created in the last exercise. For example:

Short-Term Goals:

1 Call my parents Sunday night at 5:00 p.m. and talk to them for half an hour.

(Note this as an appointment on each Sunday of the month.)

2 Invite each kid for parent/child "special time" and work with them to create something fun and age appropriate.

(Talk to your children, pick a date with each of them, and note this as an appointment at the proper date and time.)

3 Take turns researching and scheduling a date night with my partner once a month.

(Choose the first date together and be the first to do the planning. Schedule the planning time at least a week before the actual date, so that you can get tickets, organize transportation and babysitters, make reservations, etc.)

Strengthening Your Support Network

Sometimes we have a tendency to want to handle grieving in private, but it's so much easier to move through grief when you have a strong and supportive network of people in your life. People who have at least a few other people they can turn to in difficult times are less likely to become depressed or get stuck in their grief. Creating a support network can be accomplished by tapping friends, joining support groups (in person or online), cultivating more support in and among your family members, seeking spiritual guidance or support through a faith organization, or seeking therapy. If this sounds difficult, start by reaching out to the least difficult person or closest group.

With friends, think about the person who is always willing to go out for a quick cup of coffee, or who picks up the phone or texts back immediately, even when they're busy. Most people will want to help out if you say simply, honestly, and clearly something to the effect of: "Hey, you know, I've been having a hard time since I [lost my mom, got laid off, the house burned down], and I could use some live human connection. Can we talk tonight?" Don't make elaborate plans; just do something.

There are many support groups for people experiencing grief, both in person and online. They are located at nonprofits, hospitals, and through faith organizations. Sometimes, if there has been a massive loss or special set of circumstances, there will be crisis counselors who provide group counseling to a school, a workplace, or to the residents of an affected community (such as after an episode of workplace violence, a mass layoff, or a town where a large percentage of people lost their homes in a natural disaster). These groups are almost always free, form quickly, and will offer the comfort of being with other people who have experienced the same thing.

Community mental health centers also offer free and low-cost counseling for parents who have lost a child to violence, families who have lost a loved one to suicide or drug overdose, and so on. If you are faced with making arrangements following a loved one's death, a mortuary may be able to provide you with referrals. In cases of natural disaster, the Red Cross or FEMA may step in, or in the case of grief arising from the workplace, a specially trained individual from Human Resources or an Employee Assistance Program may intervene. For online support, just Google the terms that describe your situation, like "grief help group" or "group for surviving a divorce."

Cultivating more support in and among your family members may take time. And, quite often, a loss affecting the whole family will reestablish connections that have faded or will soften old, hard feelings in the light of an uncertain future. The mentality that "we're all in this together now" offers a chance to make amends, open up emotionally, become closer, and move forward. If your family is unsafe, however, or has a history of addiction or emotional or physical abuse, it's okay to rely on people other than family.

You might find yourself seeking spiritual guidance or support through a faith organization, such as a church, temple, or mosque. Reading religious or spiritual literature on your own can be a helpful connection to this community. Many spiritual organizations offer prayer circles, meditation hours, support groups, and a network of members who will call you regularly to support you through a difficult time.

You may also realize that you need more than a support group can provide and decide to seek therapy. There are grief and loss experts, or Certified Bereavement Facilitators, who are specialists trained in issues specific to grief and loss, as well as mental health issues such as depression, anxiety, and addiction. These experts can be found through referrals from family, friends, or doctors, or through online directories.

Although no one looks forward to loss or the grieving process, it can be a profound experience of expansion, strengthening, and energizing—something called post-traumatic growth. When you use the tools in this book, you are equipping yourself with the skills not only to move through your present loss, but also to deal more effectively with future losses and other difficult experiences. By making connections that strengthen your social support network, consciously choosing to live your values-focused life, and staying in the present moment, you will experience greater joy, peace, and satisfaction while moving through life's difficulties—a real accomplishment.

Resources

Books

Get Out of Your Mind and Into Your Life: The New Acceptance and Commitment Therapy, by Steven C. Hayes, PhD with Spencer Smith (New Harbinger Publications, 2005)

This is the primary do-it-yourself ACT workbook, direct from the creator himself, Dr. Hayes. It contains accessible explanations of suffering, problems with thought, willingness, and mindfulness exercises.

The Happiness Trap: How to Stop Struggling and Start Living: A Guide to ACT, by Russ Harris (Trumpeter, 2008)

A guide that explains how the way we seek happiness tends to make us miserable and fuels stress, anxiety, and depression, and offers techniques for countering self-defeating habits.

The Mindfulness and Acceptance Workbook for Depression: Using Acceptance and Commitment Therapy to Move Through Depression and Create a Life Worth Living, Second Edition, by Kirk D. Strosahl, PhD, and Patricia J. Robinson, PhD (New Harbinger Publications, 2017)

This book explains how self-compassion and mindfulness actually can reshape your brain.

The Mindfulness Workbook for Anxiety: The 8-Week Solution to Help you Manage Anxiety, Worry, and Stress, by Tanya J. Peterson, MS, NCC (Althea Press, 2018)

This book aims to help you "take back what anxiety has stolen from you" through an eight-week program of weekly challenges and daily writing exercises focusing on what's happening inside you, in the present moment.

Support Groups and Mental Health Resources

Grief in Common (griefincommon.com)
> An online community of people who share similar losses, as well as a resource for grief coaching

The National Mental Health Consumer's Self-Help Clearinghouse (MHselfhelp.org)
> An inclusive online resource connecting patients, health care providers, advocates, and policymakers

National Suicide Prevention Hotline: (800) 273-8255
> A free, 24/7/365 service, offering trained counselors who help you if you are feeling suicidal. It can also be accessed by texting TALK to 741-741.

Substance Abuse and Mental Health Services Administration (SAMHSA): (800) 662-4357
> A free, confidential helpline offering treatment referrals and information in both Spanish and English, 365 days a year

Therapy/Self-Help Resources

Association for Contextual Behavior Science (contextualscience.org)
> Offers "ACT for the Public," a resource for developing a deeper understanding of ACT, and advice for finding an ACT-trained therapist

The Happiness Trap Online Program (thehappinesstrap.com/8-week-program/)
> An 8-week online program created by Dr. Russ Harris, one of the most respected authorities on utilizing the principles of ACT to overcome stress, anxiety, and depression

Psychology Today: Find a Therapist (psychologytoday.com/us/therapists)
> A free online resource that allows you to conduct a refined search and screening if you are looking for a therapist

Grief/Bereavement Resources

American Foundation for Suicide Prevention (afsp.org)
Suicide Awareness Voices of Education (save.org)
Survivors After Suicide (afsp.org/support_group/survivors-after-suicide-13/)
Survivors of Suicide (survivorsofsuicide.com)

Grief Anonymous
> A network of supportive Facebook groups for grief and loss

HelpGuide (helpguide.org)
> Resources for mental health, grief, and loss

The National Infertility Association (resolve.org)
> Support groups for infertility and pregnancy loss

Support After Homicide (supportafterhomicide.ie)
> A free network of individuals who can help you if you are affected by loss through homicide

References

Chödrön, Pema. *When Things Fall Apart: Heart Advice for Difficult Times* (Boston, MA: Shambhala Publications, 2000).

Davis, Esther L., Frank P. Deane, and Geoffrey C. B. Lyons. "Prediction of Individual Differences in Adjustment to Loss: Acceptance and Valued-Living as Critical Appraisal and Coping Strengths." *Death Studies* 40, no. 4 (2016): 211–22. doi:10.1080/07481187.201 5.1122677.

Gawrysiak, Michael J., Stevie N. Grassetti, Jeffrey M. Greeson, Ryan C. Shorey, Ryan Pohlig, and Michael J. Baime. "The Many Facets of Mindfulness and the Prediction of Change Following Mindfulness-based Stress Reduction (MBSR)." *Journal of Clinical Psychology* 74, no. 4 (2018): 523–35. doi:10.1002/jclp.22521.

Harris, Russ. *ACT Made Simple: An Easy-to-Read Primer on Acceptance and Commitment Therapy* (Oakland, CA: New Harbinger Publications: 2019).

Hayes, Steven C. "Hello Darkness: Discovering Our Values by Confronting Our Fears" *Psychotherapy Networker* 31, no. 5 (Sept/Oct 2007): 46–52. https://www.psychotherapynetworker.org/magazine /article/625/hello-darkness.

Hayes, Steven C. "State of the ACT Evidence." Association for Contextual Behavioral Science. Accessed May 22, 2019. https://contextualscience.org/state_of_the_act_evidence.

Hayes, Steven C. "10 Signs You Know What Matters." *Psychology Today*. Last modified September 12, 2018. https://www.psychologytoday .com/us/articles/201809/10-signs-you-know-what-matters.

Hayes, Steven C. "From Loss to Love." *Psychology Today.* Last modified July 12, 2018. https://www.psychologytoday.com/us/articles/201806 /loss-love.

Hayes, Steven C. and Kal Kseib. "Why Can't We Speak to the Deepest Issues of Meaning, Love, and Loss?" *The Psychologist* 30 (May 2017): 44–47.

Hayes, Steven C. and Spencer Smith. *Get Out of Your Mind and Into Your Life: The New Acceptance and Commitment Therapy* (Oakland, CA: New Harbinger Publications, 2005).

Kabat-Zinn, Jon. *Full Catastrophe Living: Using the Wisdom of Your Body and Mind to Face Stress, Pain, and Illness.* Revised ed. (New York: Bantam Books, 2013).

Kelson, Joshua N., Mary K. Lam, Melanie Keep, and Andrew J. Campbell. "Development and Evaluation of an Online Acceptance and Commitment Therapy Program for Anxiety: Phase I Iterative Design." *Journal of Technology in Human Services* 35, no. 2 (2017): 135–51. doi:10.1080/15228835.2017.1309311.

Kropf, Nancy P., and Barbara L. Jones. "When Public Tragedies Happen: Community Practice Approaches in Grief, Loss, and Recovery." *Journal of Community Practice* 22, no. 3 (2014): 281–98. doi:10.1080/10705422.2014.929539.

Luoma, Jason B., Steven C. Hayes, and Robyn D. Walser. *Learning ACT: Second Edition: An Acceptance and Commitment Therapy Skills Training Manual for Therapists* (Oakland, CA: New Harbinger Publications, 2017).

Murakami, Haruki. *What I Talk About When I Talk About Running: A Memoir* (New York, NY: Vintage Books, 2009).

Neimeyer, Robert A., Dennis Klass, and Michael Robert Dennis. "A Social Constructionist Account of Grief: Loss and the Narration of Meaning." *Death Studies* 38, no. 8 (2014): 485–98. doi:10.1080/07481187.2014.913454.

Nhất Hạnh, Thích. *The Miracle of Mindfulness: A Manual on Meditation* (Boston, MA: Beacon Press, 1987).

Singh, Dipinti, Aeshwarya Raj, and J. S. Tripathi. "The Benefits of Mindfulness in Improving Mental Health and Well-Being." *International Journal of Social Sciences Review* 7, no. 3 (March 2019): 427–30.

Index

Acknowledgments

I am grateful for the support, passion, dedication, and education provided by my mentors and colleagues, the lessons imparted by the departed, and the affiliated programs that provide practical, accessible support for grieving individuals: Norman Farberow, PhD (1918–2015), cofounder of the Los Angeles Suicide Prevention Center, and one of the founding fathers of modern suicidology, my first mentor in the art of grief work; Alice Parsons Zulli, FT, BCPC, chaplain and founder of the Beyond Loss Grief Training Program, who furthered my education in bereavement and clinical thanatology; Survivors After Suicide, a program of Didi Hirsch Community Mental Health Center, where I learned effective brief interventions for grief; Bruce Gregory, PhD, who embedded the power of curiosity in me; and my father, for gifting me with my first journal, as well as the practice of Transcendental Meditation.

About the Author

Gretchen Kubacky, PsyD, is a health psychologist and certified bereavement facilitator who has been working with complex grief issues for more than two decades. She holds a certificate in mindfulness-based stress reduction (MBSR) and is a frequent speaker on trauma, grief and loss, men's health, and chronic and "invisible" illnesses. Dr. Kubacky is the founder of PCOSwellness.com and the author of *The PCOS Mood Cure: Your Guide to Ending the Emotional Roller Coaster.* She is also a member of the board of the Los Angeles County Psychological Association and editor of *The Los Angeles Psychologist* magazine. Dr. Kubacky lives and works in Southern California.

CPSIA information can be obtained
at www.ICGtesting.com
Printed in the USA
JSHW010939081119
2252JS00001B/1